LET ME
Grieve

BUT NOT FOREVER

To my children:
David, Shawna, and Stephen,
whose faith and courage
brought light into my darkness

I will give you the treasures of darkness,
riches stored in secret places,
so that you may know that I am the Lord,
the God of Israel, who summons you by name.

Isaiah 45:3

Unless otherwise indicated, Scripture quotations used in this book are from The Holy Bible, New International Version (NIV). Copyright © 1973, 1978, 1984 International Bible Society. Used by permission of Zondervan Bible Publishers. Other Scripture references are from the following:

> The Amplified Bible (AMP). Copyright © 1965 Zondervan Publishing House. Used by permission.
>
> The King James Version of the Bible (KJV).
>
> _The Living Bible_ (TLB), copyright 1971 by Tyndale House Publishers, Wheaton, Ill. Used by permission.
>
> The New King James Version (NKJV). Copyright © 1979, 1980, 1982, 1990, Thomas Nelson, Inc., Publisher.

Library of Congress Cataloging-in-Publication Data

Davis, Verdell, 1941–
    Let me grieve, but not forever / Verdell Davis.
        p.   cm.
    Includes Bibliographical references.
    ISBN 0-8499-1425-6
    1. Grief—Religious aspects—Christianity.   2. Widows—Religious life.   3. Grief—Religious aspects—Christianity.   4. Bereavement—Religious aspects—Christianity.   5. Consolation.   I. Title.
BV4908.5.D34   1997
248.8'66' 092—dc21   97-5643
[B]   CIP

Printed in the United States of America

7 8 9 0 1 2 3 4 9 BVG 9 8 7 6 5 4 3 2 1

LET ME

Grieve

BUT NOT FOREVER

· ·

A Journey Out of the Darkness of Loss

by Verdell Davis

WORD PUBLISHING
Dallas·London·Vancouver·Melbourne

Contents

Foreword

There are few things in this world more potent than the words of an honest human witness. Years ago, the Russian government sent a team of researchers to the United States to study what was being done about the problem of alcoholism. They visited numerous treatment centers and examined a variety of therapies. They returned home more impressed with the work of Alcoholics Anonymous than with any other group, and they reported to their superiors that the secret of this movement seemed to lie in the power of storytelling and story-listening.

They said, "One person standing up and saying simply, 'Here is how I was, here is what happened to me, and here is how I am now' appeared to have more healing impact on other struggling addicts than anything else. Such acts create the atmosphere of hope that is so crucial for the process of recovery to begin."

What Verdell Davis does in the following pages stands in that same noble tradition. Here is another powerful example of honest witness. Her life was literally turned upside down in June 1987 when a plane crash claimed the life of the husband with whom she had deeply and joyfully shared almost thirty years. That one single event suddenly raised critical issues in every facet of Verdell's life—her faith in God, her capacities to cope on her own, and the ultimate question of whether she wanted to go on living in a world so different from the one she had known.

With remarkable honesty, courage, and generosity, she shares the great variety of feelings, thoughts, and experiences that were hers as she walked, not just *into* the valley of the shadow of grief, but through it as well.

There are no quick and easy palliatives here for fellow grievers. Part of the value of this book is its utter faithfulness to all the facets and pains of losing someone who has been significant in a person's life. Verdell makes her way slowly and unevenly, as is the experience of most human mourners, but the beauty of it all is that readers can witness for themselves the growth Verdell allows to occur in her whole being. Those of us fortunate enough to read these pages will watch in wonder as Verdell comes to terms with the paradoxical awareness that she is both weaker and stronger than she once imagined.

Before this loss tragedies of this sort always seemed far removed from her—things happened to others, but she assumed they would never happen to her. After the accident she realizes that none of us is immune to suffering and that even more losses might take place. It is painful to observe the loss of innocence and the growing awareness of vulnerability that takes deeper root in this one who had never before really been, as she says, "a person of sorrow, acquainted with grief." But at the same time Verdell begins to discover things about herself that she had never known before. She chronicles how it slowly dawned on her that she could survive in the world without the support and companionship of her beloved husband. She also comes to realize that she has a good mind and can think out the hard theological dilemmas she had always left up to her minister husband.

It is heartwarming to witness the recognition growing in her that she is a stronger person than she had ever thought. What a few years before had seemed impossible, she now finds herself doing and doing well. Her own graphic image of this process is that "surviving gave way to living again."

To her genuine amazement and because of her own courage and the grace of God, she does make it *through* the valley of the shadow of grief and emerges a very different human being from the one thrust into that ravine *seven* years before. Just as fractured bones are said to grow back stronger at the broken places, so Verdell Davis stands at the end of the book as a stronger believer and coper and carer than ever before.

Her honest witness has the ability to create an atmosphere of hope in which the process of recovery can begin for others. Hobart Mowrer is right: "You alone can do your grief work, but then again, you cannot do it alone." I predict that through this book, Verdell Davis will accompany many "to the Light on the other side" of the valley of bereavement.

John R. Claypool
Birmingham, Alabama

Acknowledgments

It is impossible for me to adequately thank those who have cared, encouraged, prayed, and listened while I alternately exuded excitement and joy at the very thought of writing and lapsed into utter dismay at my lack of faith when the going got tough. It is to those who believed in me when I didn't believe in myself that I owe a great debt of gratitude as I write the final words of this book. And all of you who told me of your prayers for me during this project, please know that you have a special place in my heart.

There are some I must acknowledge who met particular needs in moving this dream into reality. . . *Bob DeMoss*—who gave me the push I needed to get those first chapters written for the editoral board to consider; *Jeff Pistor* and *Major and Bonnie Lytton*—who labored hard to move me from computer illiteracy to some measure of competency; *Dewey and Virginia Presley*—who gave me unlimited use of their lake house where I could write to my heart's content and watch the sun set at the same time; *my family*—who understood when I kept disappearing, but who are ready for this project to be finished; *Nancy Norris*—who long ago became my friend, whose encouragement and direction in this endeavor have been priceless, and whose quick sense of humor I have needed; *Kip Jordon*—who believed in me all along; *Allen Townes*—who read each chapter as I finished it and gave me constant encouragement and invaluable feedback; *J'Nell Green*—who came in on the tedious details; *Sue Ann Jones*—who gave her polishing touches to this first time author's manuscript; and *Lynn Vanderzalm*—who kept me from giving up when I was sure I had nothing to say after all.

And to the others whose names are written indelibly into my life, my thanks for your immeasurable gifts to me.

Before My
Own Lifestorm . . .

Many times I read in the morning paper or watched on the evening news some tragedy that engulfed someone—or many someones—in the devastating realities of loss and pain and grief, and along with the fear such stories struck deep down inside of me was the unacknowledged belief, *These things happen to other people.*

What did I know of that kind of lifestorm? I well remember putting my arms around a dear friend just a couple of hours after her husband had died of a sudden heart attack and saying, "Oh, Sybil, I have no idea how you feel."

Many times I read a story of how someone had overcome a lifestorm and had found new depths of awareness and faith and joy, then I questioned if I could ever survive anything like that, much less be triumphant through it. I remember thinking oftentimes when I read such a story that I would like to have that strength of spirit but I did not want to pay the price it seemed to require.

Many times I read in the Scriptures or listened to the Word being expounded or even taught it myself, that the God we could trust in the sunshine of our days was the same God we could trust in the darkness of our nights, and so often I wondered if I would still believe this promise when the "valley of the shadow" threatened everything precious to me and the light was barely visible.

I remember standing before the group of high school seniors I was teaching as we talked about the goodness and faithfulness and trustworthiness of our God, who loves us with an unfailing love. I said to them, "You know, I believe what I'm telling you with everything in me. But I have not yet been in a situation that severely tested my faith. I know that time will come for me someday, and I am sure then I will have some new things to tell you."

That time did come. Less than six months later, my husband's death was the tragedy in the news, and my picture was the one under the headline. This was not happening to someone else. I was struck by a lifestorm that would bring me face to face with everything I believed and everything I had ever been taught. This book is the result of that journey.

It is not my purpose here to chronicle all the events that make up my story but to share just those particulars that will enable you to make sense of the personal nature of this writing. There were four men in the airplane crash that took my husband's life, so the story itself belongs to all these families as well as to the myriad of friends that felt their losses very deeply.

In these last seven years I have become well acquainted with the pain, despair, and grief that come with the loss of a spouse, and at the same time I have, through the experiences of others who have let me be a part of their life journeys, learned of other kinds of losses. In these pages I will share with you very honestly the emptiness, the questions, and the fears that have plagued my steps, but I will also tell you of the hope that anchored my soul when there was no desire to go on living. And I must ask of you, as I ask of the audiences when I speak, "Please don't hear me say that my pain is greater than your pain, or my loss greater than your loss." Pain is a great common denominator, and we each need God's very special grace to teach us not to lean on the things of this world but on the unshakable kingdom of God.

It is my desire as you read this book that you will find yourself less reading my story and more getting in touch with your own.

The Families

I walked in a Dallas cemetery one morning and stood at the graves of three friends killed in an airplane accident: George L. Clark, chairman of the board and CEO of MBank in Dallas; Dr. Trevor E. Mabery, an ear, nose, and throat surgeon who was instrumental in helping to found Humana Hospital-Medical City in Dallas; Hugo W. Schoellkopf III, entrepreneur, sporting goods manufacturer, and owner and developer of Elk Canyon Ranch, a guest ranch in Montana. All were highly respected in their professional fields, strong in their ever-growing Christian commitment, and deeply devoted to their families. I was late in grieving for these friends because my husband, Creath Davis, was killed in the same accident. I grieved first for him.

As I spent some time at each grave I let my mind wander through memories of how our families had become friends, of hunting and fishing trips taken together, of laughter and tears as we shared life's ups and downs, of Bible studies and weddings and funerals, and of encouraging each other in raising our children to love the Lord in the midst of a degenerating society.

As I considered my own thoughts and feelings, my own tears and joys, my own perceptions of events surrounding that airplane crash, and my own struggles in the valley of despair, I knew most assuredly that the other three wives wrestled with their anguish just as I did with mine. I had watched the courage and faith of my children as they found their way in young adulthood without their strong father in their lives, and I knew the other children who lost their fathers had shown the same courage and faith and also had struggled with the issues of lives altered too soon by such a loss. I thought of my grandchildren, who would never have the joy of hearing their grandfather's laughter. I knew of Will and Justin Schoellkopf, the youngest of the children in these four families, growing up without their father to play with them, teach them, and guide them into manhood.

Our friendship continues to make us a part of each other's lives now just as we had been before a very public tragedy swept us beyond the scope of private grief. Our friendship still brings comfort and encouragement as we embrace life again with wonder at the things God has brought us through and with anticipation of what life holds for us now.

Let me introduce you to these friends . . .

Ann and George Clark spent a great deal of their time and energies building memories with their three sons. They were intricately involved in their boys' lives, from their school activities, to teaching them the finer points of the game of golf, to family hunting and fishing expeditions and camping trips. George coached their sports teams, and Ann was a devoted fan. Ann and George regularly opened their warm, loving home to gatherings of folks who wanted to learn about the things of God, about parenting with love and honor, and about the ways of being God's people in a hurting world.

Ann has a gift for embracing people into her life and her home, and her love of others seems to flow back to her from every direction. She and I have traveled many of the same trails in these last seven years. We have been able to encourage each other as we both sought the wisdom of a gifted counselor to help each of us deal with some issues that were holding us back from living our lives with the freedom and excitement God offers to his children.

Two of her three boys were still at home at the time of the accident, and Ann leaned heavily on the things she had learned through years of walking with God as she guided David and Andy into young adulthood. The oldest son,

George, and his wife, Ashley, now live in Houston. David, a recent college graduate, lives and works in Dallas. Andy is a junior in college, majoring in business. All the boys have carried forth their father's love for sports and the outdoors, and all three of them have inherited their parents' love for laughter and friends.

Lucy and Trevor Mabery were usually surrounded by throngs of singles who leaned on their leadership as they traversed the challenging terrain of living as Christians in an era of fading moral values. The Maberys' home and their hearts were open to youth groups, seminary students, medical colleagues, and friends of any age—and those who came went away encouraged and blessed by the spiritual maturity of this couple.

Trevor was highly respected by his peers and adored by his patients, and Lucy has for many years been known as a gifted Bible teacher. She has now completed both a master of theology degree and a Ph.D. in marriage and family counseling and is a professor at Dallas Theological Seminary.

But Lucy's delight has always been her children. Her daughter, Janet, is an audiologist, and Janet's husband, Paul Fulmer, followed in his father-in-law's footsteps and is now an otolaryngologist in Tyler, Texas. They have two of Lucy's three grandchildren, Catharine and Lauren.

The Maberys' older son, Dan, married ten days before he lost his father. He is now in law school, and he and his wife, Cheryl, have Lucy's third granddaughter, Madeline. Lucy's youngest, Stephen, graduated from Baylor University and is working in the real estate business. He and my son Stephen share a house in Dallas with another Baylor friend. Two other Stephens with a greater passion for hunting and fishing you will not find!

Gail and Hugo Schoellkopf met at one of Creath's Bible studies and quickly grew to appreciate each other's sensitivity to the spiritual journey each of them was on. Gail found in Hugo both the depth of character and the Christian commitment she had prayed for, and their marriage of nine years brought great joy into her life. Shortly after they were married, Gail's brother, Tommy Obenchain, came to live with them, and he found Hugo to be a strong and vital influence in his life. Tommy and my son David have shared a lot of experiences as friends through high school, through their college years (even though they were separated by different schools), through the days of searching for a missing airplane and the events that followed, and now as young adults with families of their own. Tommy and his wife, Beth, have two boys and are expecting their third child soon.

Gail has the youngest family and has sought God's will and guidance every step of the way as a mother suddenly alone with two little boys, Will and Justin. The boys were young enough at the time of their father's death that their memories of him have been enhanced by the legacy of his warm and loving spirit that Gail has imparted to them. I well remember those last days at Elk Canyon Ranch in 1987 before Gail and her boys, and Shawna, Stephen, and I came back to Dallas before the men began to arrive for the Focus on the Family retreat. I watched Hugo ride his horse with three-year-old Justin snuggled safely into the saddle with him; and I saw Hugo glow with pride as he rode beside Will, who at seven was learning to handle his own horse quite well. These memories were captured in photographs for them. Will is now fourteen, loves playing basketball for his school's team, and reminds all of us of his father. Justin is now ten and already shows much of his dad's spirit with his quick sense of humor and his sensitive heart.

And let me introduce you to *my* family: Our oldest son, David, fills his life with many ministry involvements, at the same time he holds a position with a major Dallas corporation. He and his lovely wife, Shelley, are the parents of my three precious grandchildren: Brittany, Will, and Sara Beth. Our daughter, Shawna, teaches first grade in Dallas and was recently married to John Wooley, who is busy establishing his own company.

And Stephen, our youngest, is an operations manager for a national relocation corporation, but ranching is his first love.

Friends we were, and friends we are. Perhaps Gail said it best as we were readying to leave her house for the first of four burials: "Our lives are inextricably linked together." In some ways I feel amiss that I have not included them more in the body of this book, but at the same time I know I cannot tell you their stories. I can only tell you mine.

1

Rogue Winds
and Rainbows

When you pass through the waters,
I will be with you;
and when you pass through the rivers,
they will not sweep over you.
When you walk through the fire,
you will not be burned;
the flames will not set you ablaze.

Isaiah 43:2

O joy that seekest me through pain,
I cannot close my heart to thee;
I trace the rainbow through the rain,
And feel the promise is not vain
That morn shall tearless be.

George Matheson
"O Love That Will
Not Let Me Go"

P*lease, God. Please don't tell me my greatest fear has come true!* I begged God as I paced the backyard so my twenty-one-year-old daughter, back in the house, could not see me shaking.

The plane should have been home hours ago.

As I paced I began remembering flashes of conversations Creath and I had had recently, conversations he had started with, *"If anything should ever happen to me . . ."* I shook my head and cried aloud, *"No, God! Please, NO!"*

The morning of June 28, 1987, had started bright and expectantly, full of anticipation of Creath's coming home. My life was much as I would have chosen it to be. I had a minister husband I adored, three grown children, a precious granddaughter and a five-week-old grandson named after his grandfather. I enjoyed a profession that gave me a great sense of accomplishment and good health that I never took for granted. I was content.

That evening was a different story. I was with three other wives, making phone calls to alert the proper authorities that the private plane carrying our husbands had not arrived from Montana. Fear gripped our hearts, but hope cleared our minds enough so we could do the things that had to be done. Friends began to pour in, and shortly before midnight the first of many private planes and corporate jets left Dallas for Montana. The search had begun.

Somehow we made it through the night by staying together, and the next morning I hugged my two grown sons as they, too, left aboard yet another corporate jet with some of the other sons to join in the search for their fathers. As my daughter, my daughter-in-law, and I embraced these young men and whispered prayers for their safety, every muscle in my body ached terribly from the intensity of each passing moment.

Later that day the crowd that had gathered at one of the homes stood in front of the television, silent in our disbelief. Flashed on the screen were the pictures of the four men. We listened as the newscaster told of their faith and friendship and of their returning together from a Focus on the Family men's retreat at a ranch in Montana. He described the Cessna 421, saying that the small, private plane was presumed down in the mountainous region of the Montana-Wyoming border. He told of the massive air search that was being mounted, and as the cameras scanned the Billings airport headquarters I saw my two sons heading for one of the planes on the runway. The pain in my heart at that moment has no words.

I wanted to scream, "This can't be happening!" and I knew the other wives standing there were thinking the same. The friends surrounding us were stunned at the thought of losing four of their friends at one time—the pain was on their faces. We all needed each other.

As Monday turned into Tuesday we kept our vigil by the phones and the television. Calls were coming in from all over the country as the search began to attract attention far beyond our community. We tried to comfort hurting friends even as they tried to comfort us. Food and flowers and telegrams reassured us we were not alone. We hugged and cried, laughed and prayed, encouraged and consoled, read from the Scriptures and clung to the promises that in our weakness he is strong and that his grace would be sufficient. The lives of those four men, and indeed of all of us were in his sovereign hands.

Tuesday became Wednesday, and someone handed me the *Dallas Morning News*. The front-page lead story carried a picture of my daughter, my daughter-in-law, and me sitting in a church beside one of the ministers at a large gathering for prayer the night before. The article said authorities held out little hope. I looked at that picture and read those headlines and felt the life drain out of me.

This was not happening to someone else.

The telephone call came as all the wives, our children who had not gone to Montana, and many of our friends were together at one home. The wives and a few others went into a smaller room and sat around a speaker phone as the message came: The plane has been found. It is a positive identification. It is about ten thousand feet up on a mountain peak just outside Cody, Wyoming.

There are no survivors.

Rogue wind. The sailors' term describes a wind that comes with no warning out of a clear blue sky, blows across a placid sea, and in moments is gone, leaving devastation in its wake. That is the storm that blew across my life on June 28, 1987. A storm with no warning on a day of sunshine and happy thoughts. A storm that forever changed my life.

But just as I look back and see the rogue wind, I must also see the rainbows that appeared in my gray and cloudy skies and etched my horizons with the assurance that God would walk through the storm with me.

Storms come in many forms. Some, indeed, come with no warning. Some we see brewing and know it is only a matter of time. The storm may be the death of a spouse, a child, a parent, a very dear friend. It may be the loss of health or the loss of a home to flood or fire. It might be financial reversals that take away the security and comforts we had grown so accustomed to, or a major move that takes us away from the familiar and the loved. The storm may be family or relational crises that sever the ties that bind us to one another, leaving us with bleeding emotional wounds.

Whenever a storm blows into our lives, it brings along its own store of heartaches; and all pain, from whatever source, is an intensely personal experience. Most often we cannot choose what happens to us—our choice lies in what we do with what life brings our way. Will we see only the devastation left by the rogue wind, or will we also see the rainbows that promise life will not always feel so oppressive?

The pains, the heartaches, the losses of our lives can become the altar on which we offer up to God all the things that keep us relying on our own strength. It is then that God can truly do a new work in us and show us himself in ways we have never seen before.

So, when we find ourselves being forced to walk in a way we did not choose and to shoulder a burden we are sure we cannot bear, what do we do? Where do we turn? How do we stay steady in the storm? What is the hope of our faith?

Lord, the storms come, and we cry out in our agony that life is unfair. We doubt your love and question your goodness. And the pain often blinds us to the rainbows of your presence.

The fear that life will never be good again keeps us clinging to the shreds of what we had instead of allowing you to build a new and deeper life out of our brokenness.

Help us, Father, to remember in these dark days the things we know to be true about you, the things that seem so easy to believe when life feels good.

Help us to cling tenaciously to the promises that your love is unfailing, your strength is made known in our weakness, and you will never leave us or forsake us.

Give us the grace to offer up to you our tear-stained praises for being our anchor in the storm.

Amen

2
Light for the Next Step

Blessed are those who have learned to acclaim you,
who walk in the light of your presence, O Lord.

Psalm 89:15

What will we do in the midnight of our need, when the light of
life is gone, when our personal cupboards are despairingly
bare? . . . If we have come often to God in the sunshine of our
lives, our anxious feet will find the familiar pathway, even in
the darkest night. Though blinded by disaster, though hounded
and hindered by doubt, though confused by life which seems
out of hand, we can find our way to God intuitively because
going to Him has become second nature, a way of life.

Richard Exley
The Other God

I read that in the monasteries of ancient Europe the monks
walked the dark hallways with candles secured to the toes
of their shoes, giving light only for the next step.

Never one to step out bravely into the dark and unknown,
when I first read about those monks I shivered at the thought of
seeing no more than the space a tiny little candle could illuminate. But then I began to remember just how much light a match,
a candle, an oil lamp, a fireplace, can give in a darkened room.

Back came the memory of going to Longhorn Cavern as a
child growing up in Central Texas. I shivered in fear as all the
lights were turned off on our band of sightseers hundreds of feet

underground; then, wonder of wonders, when the guide lit one match it seemed as if the sun had suddenly come into that cave. I remember his saying, "All the darkness in the world cannot put out light, but one little match can push back the darkness."

And back came the special memories of spending time at my grandparents' farm before electricity had made it to the far reaches of the rural area where they lived. I remember being fascinated by the light of the kerosene lamps. I learned about keeping the lamps filled with oil and about keeping the wicks trimmed and the globes clean. In that same farmhouse I came to love the flickering of the fireplace as the fire was dying down for the night, the shadows dancing around the room as the flames fluttered and hissed.

These memories let me see the gift of the candles to those monks going about their service to God in those cold, dark monasteries and to grasp the meaning of light for the next step—as they walked, the light always went just before them.

I did not know it then, but now I know that there are many kinds of darkness. And the light needed is not always so simple as a match burning a moment in a dark cave. Shattered dreams, broken relationships, lost hopes, or the death of a loved one is the kind of darkness that robs even the sun of its warmth. It is a darkness that often renders us blind as we close our eyes against the awfulness of the black void that surrounds us, hoping that when we open our eyes again the darkness will have disappeared.

"Blacker than a hundred midnights, down in a cypress swamp." So go the words in *God's Trombones,* James Weldon Johnson's classic poem about creation. Having memorized that poem so very long ago, those words were etched in my mind, and they came closer to describing the indescribable agony I felt than anything else I could think of. The black of a hundred midnights had been closing in for seven days now. The candles and the oil lamps and the fire in the fireplace had all gone out for me, and I felt very vulnerable to the menacing darkness.

The plane crash that took my husband's life and the lives of three very close friends happened on a Sunday. God indeed gave His very special grace to us all to get through three days of searching for the plane, through the arrangements that had to be made on Thursday for four unexpected deaths, and through three burials and a memorial service in Dallas on Friday attended by thousands of mourners. Then, on Saturday, there was one more funeral . . . Creath's.

My husband and I had both been raised in the same small farming and ranching community in central Texas and had long known that we would be buried there in the same cemetery as my father and grandfather and Creath's grandparents. Creath had always been the "favorite son" of this small town, especially of the church he had preached in many times. I knew the people there who had followed the event closely on the television news and had moved to comfort Creath's parents and my mother needed their chance to be part of the loss and grief.

That Saturday was July 4, the end of a very long week. It never occurred to me to ask the other families to go with me to Comanche for the funeral after all we had been through, but I found that it never occurred to them not to go. The other wives and all the older children made the three-hour trip, as did about sixty other friends from Dallas and other parts of the state.

When I walked into the sanctuary of the First Baptist Church that day and saw the casket down front, the reality of all that had happened caved in on me. It was the first time I had been in the presence of the body, and I learned at that moment how much a part of closure it is to be able to see the body. Of course, circumstances of this death precluded that, but at least I could touch the casket. I feel so for those who lose loved ones in a situation where the body is never found.

I had moved through the day as if following a script, doing all the things expected, with just enough light to see the step in front of me. After visiting with the people at the graveside and back at the church for quite some time after the funeral, my two sons, my daughter, my daughter-in-law, my eighteen-month-old granddaughter, and my new grandson got into the Suburban to make the long trip back to Dallas. There was no script for tomorrow, or the many tomorrows to come.

Somewhere along the way the heaviness became more than I could bear. I felt myself standing at the entrance to a very deep, very dark tunnel, and I didn't want to go in. I kept trying to turn around and go back, but there was nothing behind me. My life as I had known it was not there for me to go back to. I knew I had no choice but to walk through all the pain and heartache and questions and dark despair that were in that tunnel. And at that moment I felt no assurance that I would ever come out on the other side a whole person. The tears flowed down my cheeks as my family quietly chatted around me; then the pure exhaustion of an incomprehensible tragedy overwhelmed me, and I fell asleep.

The tunnel was dark indeed—and endless. Each morning I awoke and found myself still surrounded by darkness. Taking care of menial tasks required enormous effort. Trying to stay with a conversation was sometimes beyond me—I would be in the middle of a sentence and forget what I was saying. In fact, remembering anything seemed like a miracle. And trying to talk to lawyers and insurance representatives who were working with me on estate matters had to be as challenging for them as it was for me. I know I asked them the same questions over and over—I never knew if I didn't understand the answer or just couldn't remember it.

At least now I can look back with a bit of amusement at the way I finally tackled a very large stack of letters, insurance forms, estate questionnaires, and unpaid bills. For several weeks I had put everything that didn't demand an immediate reply on my kitchen table, and eventually I simply covered it all with a sheet. Out of sight out of mind, I suppose. Then one morning I knew the monster under the sheet was going to attack me if I didn't attack it first. So I sat down at the table and cried real tears of anger and frustration and loneliness for a while. Eventually I raised my head and said, "Okay, Lord. I'm a fairly bright girl. I'm going to take this sheet off this table and open one envelope. If I can make any sense out of whatever is inside it, I will open another one. If not, I am going to put the sheet back on the table and go back to bed."

I know now that even that bit of levity was a little extra light for that particular step. Back then, I wanted to already know how to take care of all the details. I wanted to feel confident about the monumental, daily decisions I was having to make. I wanted to have at least some clue that the steps in front of me were surmountable. I wanted the path to be flooded with light. And yet, it was with small flickers of candle glow that God kept gently reminding me, "My grace is sufficient." I only needed light for one envelope, one conversation, one decision, one step at a time.

Sometimes God sends the brilliant light of a rainbow to remind us of his presence, lest we forget in our personal darkness his great and gracious promises to never leave us alone. One such rainbow was seen by hundreds of friends visiting outside the church after the late afternoon memorial service and became part of the live evening newscast when it was captured by a cameraman and commented on by the reporter. The day was a hot, clear July 3, not a day for rainbows, but there it was, cupped upward in the few wispy clouds in a very blue sky. It seems the rainbow had been there for over an hour.

A picture given to us a few weeks later told the rest of the story, a story shared widely by Dr. James Dobson of Focus on the Family, who was one of the friends standing outside the church that afternoon. He recently included in his book, *When God Doesn't Make Sense,* the picture taken about the time the memorial service was beginning by a young mother who had stayed home with her own and a friend's children. As amazed as we were at how long the rainbow remained there, we were more amazed to see in the picture, cradled, it seemed, in the upturned rainbow, the dark form of a small airplane that had been flying in the area at the time, completely unnoticed by the one taking the picture.

After the plane crash we became acutely aware of rainbows, grateful for their beauty and their symbolism of God's faithfulness to His promises. A few weeks later, Gail Schoellkopf and I watched a double rainbow form as we stood on the mountain in Montana where we had last been with our husbands, and we felt encouragement that we had seen this spectacular reminder at this particular time and place.

Another rainbow appeared outside our airplane window as the other wives—Ann, Gail, and Lucy—and I flew to California to be involved in a dedication ceremony at Focus on the Family. Seeing rainbows from an airplane is not unusual, but none of us had seen one before.

Rainbows became a part of our healing and of our learning to trust God to lead us when the steps ahead lay in the shadows. Our friends Bob and Linda Buford, who had lost their only child, twenty-four-year-old Ross, in a drowning accident just five months before the airplane accident claimed four of their friends, wrote us a note, describing rainbows as God's wonderful caring providence saying to all of us, "I know life doesn't seem to make sense for you now, but I care for you. I am in control, and in due course I will show you how these small chips of life fit together in the huge mosaic I have crafted."

As time went on I began to be more and more aware of the ways God was bringing light into my dark days. Gradually, I found myself "cursing the darkness" less and moving toward the light more. I began to see rainbow colors in the hugs of friends, the offer of someone to help with a particular need, the unexpected phone call of encouragement when I thought I wouldn't make it through the night, the dawning of new insight into the ways of God with his hurting children.

Even as I wondered why God could not light the way a little more brightly when we are so consumed with pain and fear, when we are paralyzed by the overwhelming number of things to be done and the intensity of emotions accompanying every decision, even then I knew the answer. *God would have us trust him.* Just trust him.

Trust him to know our way much better than we ever could, even if our paths were exposed to all the light possible.

Trust him to give us the light we need.

Trust him to teach us his utter faithfulness.

Trust him to do a far greater work in our lives than we have ever dreamed.

Trust him to be there in our darkness.

In teaching us to walk by faith and not by sight, God is placing down deep inside of us the resources we will need when darkness overtakes our journey. But more, he is seeking to forge in us a faith that will, in turn, make us lights to others in the sadness of their journey.

And so I have learned in this journey that the candle on the toe of each shoe is really enough. Because God himself is the candle.

Lord, when the way is dark
 We ask,
  we plead,
   we beg for more light.
We shrink back from the path so dimly lit.
We would rather trust our eyes than your hand.

When a lifestorm has left our way treacherous
We need you to guide us through.
The light may be comforting,
But our vision is limited.
Your vision, Lord, is not.

You see the end from the very beginning
*   and the present in light of the future,*
*   the past in perspective of a bigger picture.*
We are bound by time and space,
*   by pain and fear*
*   and hopes and dreams*
*   and joys and sorrows,*
By what we can see and taste and touch and feel.

Release us.
Touch us with your spirit.
May the rainbow colors of your grace to us
*   not be lost in our fear of the dark,*
And let us not so desire the brilliance of the sun
*   that we miss the glow of your candles.*
*   Amen*

3
Strong in the
Broken Places

We have this treasure in jars of clay to show that this all-surpassing power is from God and not from us. We are hard pressed on every side, but not crushed; perplexed, but not in despair; persecuted, but not abandoned; struck down, but not destroyed. . . . Therefore we do not lose heart. . . . My grace is sufficient for you, for my power is made perfect in weakness.

2 Corinthians 4:7–9,
16; 12:9

The very fire that blackens my horizons warms my soul. The darkness that oppresses my mind sharpens my vision. The flood that overwhelms my heart quenches my thirst. The thorns that penetrate my flesh strengthen my spirit. The grave that buries my desires deepens my devotion. Man's failure to comprehend this intention of God is one of life's true calamities.

James Means
A Tearful Celebration

Can strength be born out of weakness? Courage out of fear? Joy out of sorrow? Confidence out of feelings of inadequacy? Compassion out of pain? New life out of loss? Can our brokenness teach us more about ourselves, more about God's faithfulness, and more about the temporal nature of these lives we are living?

The answer to all these questions is a resounding, "Yes!" But the word *can* indicates it is not necessarily a sure outcome. In any life-altering suffering and trial, the danger of becoming angry, disillusioned, and bitter or of becoming lethargic and succumbing to fatalism is very real. I discovered that you can be quite philosophical about pain—until the pain is yours. It is much easier to give platitudes about how to survive loss and heartache before you have your own. The way remains uncharted for each of us, and the path is strewn both with opportunities for growth and temptations for escape.

We live in a world gone wrong, one that was created perfect but now suffers the ravages of sin: death, violated relationships, children born with disabilities and deformities, disease, man's inhumanity to man, moral failures, tragedies of major proportions, chaos. It is, indeed, a broken world. But it is one thing to shake our heads at the mess the world is in; it is quite another to confront the reality of it in our own lives. One layer away, it is sad. But when it hits *us,* it is ominous. Out there, it is frightening. Inside, it is terrifying. When we are touched deeply and personally by the unfairness in a fallen world, we are shocked that such a thing could actually be happening to us. And we want the quickest way out.

Suffering comes to the rich and the poor, the learned and the unlearned, the strong and the weak, the believer and the nonbeliever, the loved and the unloved, the faithful and the unfaithful, the young and the old. To all.

Suffering is intensely personal and as unique as each sufferer. Though we may endure the same disease or broken relationship or disability or failure, trying to compare sufferings is to ignore the unique dynamics of each individual life. Just to listen to the stories in an AA meeting, where all are brought together by their common addiction to alcohol, is to find that each pain, each heartache, each loss, each interplay of relationships, is highly charged with some twist no one else in the room has experienced in quite the same way. It is to find that indeed no two sufferings are the same.

Likewise, brokenness comes from many sources: A marriage that cannot stand the test of time and life-stresses. A divorced parent who must visit his or her children on a schedule someone else prescribes. A friend or business associate who betrays trust. Children who rebel in a hundred different ways. Financial security that is stripped away by unwise business moves or by uncontrollable economic factors. Physical illness or disability that dictates one's way of living. A sinful act with far-reaching consequences. Unfulfilled desire for the companionship of a mate or the gift of a child. The final acceptance that a long-held dream will never come true. The death of one who gave your life its glow and beauty.

Though sweeping in statement, the brokenness produced by lifestorms such as these is specific, personal, and oh, so painful. We each must claim our own suffering. We must resist seeing our own sorrows as either more devastating or less important than someone else's. Mine are unique to me, and if I am ever going to deal with them honestly and openly, I must accept that what is going on in my life deserves my respect, whether it be a storm from without or one I brought on by unwise or wrongful choices.

When we stand in the middle of a lifestorm, it seems as if the storm has become our way of life. We cannot see a way out. We are unable to chart a course back to smoother waters. We feel defeated—and broken. Will that brokenness produce a cynicism that will keep us forever in the mire of "if only" thinking? Or will we yield up that brokenness to the resources of One who calms the winds and the waves, heals the brokenhearted, and forgives the most grievous of sins? The choice is ours.

There is risk in great loss, risk that the loss will become a wedge we use to push away a God we cannot understand. I feared this for my children. I knew they each had made a commitment to the God they had come to know as they grew up, but I knew, too, that their faith was young and tender.

In the swirl of activity surrounding the search for the missing plane I prayed intensely that these children would see God's hand in this event in their lives, whatever the outcome of the search. I prayed for David and Stephen and the other sons in Montana during the search for the plane and especially for Shawna, waiting here and refusing to even entertain the thought that her dad would not be found alive. I feared the most for her.

I prayed all the more when I had to put my arms around her and tell her that the plane had been found and that her dad was dead. I agonized through her cries of "No, I don't believe it!" And I felt such stabs of pain for her two brothers when they called before leaving to come home and said, "Mom, we'll all be all right."

Three days later we were together in the church where their dad's funeral was to be held. I walked over to the side of the sanctuary to talk with the minister for a moment, and when I turned back I saw my three children kneeling in front of the casket, each of the boys with an arm around their sister between them. I walked over and stood behind them and listened as they prayed. They asked God to give them the kind of love for him that their dad had had. Their words brought a flood of tears to my heart, tears of pain for their loss and gratitude for their faith. My prayer—that God would use this experience in their lives as a wedge to push them closer to him and not let such a tragic, untimely loss cause them to see him as less than loving—was being answered.

In the days immediately following the funeral, what I saw in my own children was enough to make me believe that God truly can make us stronger than we would ever have dreamed possible through the brokenness that drives us to our knees. I saw these three young adults reach down into the inner recesses of their young lives and pull to the surface courage and strength they did not know they had. The confusion and despair they felt in losing their father in such a tragic, untimely way forced upon them some heavy choices—but choices they each had to make down inside where no one could see, and no one could go, and no one could help. They each had to make these choices alone. What would they do with the pain? What would they do with the questions? What would they do with God?

That summer saw a parade of young people through our home. They would eat pizza or popcorn or cookies and sit on the floor and talk about what had happened and try to relate this tragedy with what they had been taught in Sunday school all their lives. I listened intently to them all, but especially to mine as they would say, "Sure, we don't understand this, but does that mean God isn't good? What does he want us to learn out of all this?" And I cried as I listened to my son Stephen challenge them more than once with the words of his dad: "Let's pledge ourselves to ask God to give us a love for him and his purpose that runs deeper than anything else in our lives, no matter what happens."

Then the time came for Shawna and Stephen to go back to college. And neither of them wanted to leave the support we, as a family, had come to be for each other. They dreaded going back and seeing friends they had not seen since the accident and having to feel their awkwardness in that first encounter. They could not imagine finding enough mental focus or interest to concentrate on academic studies. And they did not want to leave me alone. It was a wrenching apart of a family bonded by pain, but a wrenching that had to happen.

David and I went with Shawna to her school in West Texas and left her crying in the doorway of her dorm. The next day I stood in my kitchen window and watched Stephen lay his head on the steering wheel of his truck for ever so long, knowing that if I walked out there he would come back in to stay and take care of me. Weak and pitiful cries for help went up from our tear-choked hearts many times during the weeks and months to come as we continually battled the seemingly impossible. And even as we each did the things we knew we must, we could not be certain we would make it through one whole day.

Without the strong father they had come to rely on, without his being there at the very center of all of our family activities, without his wisdom to draw from, they had to piece together for themselves how they would deal with the issues that were now theirs alone. We still talked many things over as a family, and they still made many long, late-night phone calls to me, but inside they began to feel a different level of responsibility than they had anticipated. At many turns in the road I saw them choose again and again, in spite of their questions with no answers and in the midst of many tears, to believe that God had a purpose for all that happens in their lives and to trust him to give them the strength and courage they needed for the journey.

"When it comes to putting broken lives back together," Frederick Buechner wrote, "the human best tends to be at odds with the holy best. To do for yourself the best that you have it in you to do—to grit your teeth and clench your fists in order to survive the world at its harshest and worst—is, by that very act, to be unable to let something be done for you and in you that is more wonderful still."[1]

To become strong in the broken places in our lives demands that we do two things, seeming opposites: hang in there, and let go. To somehow dig up the courage to keep going is the very courage that allows us to scoop up the broken pieces of our lives and lay them all at the feet of One who would do more in us than just get us through the storm. As James Means said, he would take the fire that blackens our horizons and warm our souls with it. He would sharpen our vision in the darkness that oppresses us. He would use the despair of standing at a grave to deepen our trust. This we cannot do for ourselves. Perhaps because our brokenness brings us to the end of ourselves, it is here, in these jars of clay that we offer up to his very special grace, that God's all-surpassing power is made known and he, indeed, makes us strong in our broken places.

> *Lord,*
> *None of us would choose brokenness.*
> *We want to be strong and self-reliant,*
> *and even unbreakable.*
>
> *But Lord*
> *No matter how tall we stand on our own,*
> *We are weak and vulnerable in the face of life's tragedies*
> *and sorrows,*
> *And we are scared.*
>
> *And so, Lord,*
> *When one of life's calamities*
> *Leaves us with only fragments of what we once knew,*
> *We struggle to piece our life back together, like some*
> *giant puzzle.*
> *And you let us,*
> *If that is what we insist upon.*
>
> *But you would do a greater work in us,*
> *You would take the broken pieces*
> *And infuse them with new life*
> *and bind them up with your grace,*
> *And give us back*
> *strength for our weakness*
> *courage for our fear*
> *joy for our sorrow*
> *forgiveness for our failings.*
>
> *Use us,*
> *Jars of clay that we are,*

To show forth your all-surpassing power.
Touch us and heal us
      and make us strong in our broken places.
Do in us what we cannot do for ourselves.
                              Amen

— 4
Questions Job and I Asked

I desire to speak to the Almighty and to argue my case with God. . . . I would find out what he would answer me, and consider what he would say. . . . Surely I spoke of things I did not understand, things too wonderful for me to know. . . . My ears had heard of you but now my eyes have seen you.

Job 13:3; 23:5; 42:3, 5

One bold message in the book of Job is that you can say anything to God. Throw at him your grief, your anger, your doubt, your bitterness, your betrayal, your disappointment—he can absorb them all. As often as not, spiritual giants of the Bible are shown contending with God. They prefer to go away limping, like Jacob, rather than to shut God out.

Philip Yancey
Disappointment with God

Job was not my favorite book in the Bible. I found it very hard to read about all that suffering. I think I was afraid I might find my faith being tested someday and wouldn't pass the test. I knew enough about Job to know he said some profound things about God in his many discourses with his three friends and he also brought to God the bitterness and betrayal he felt at the way God was handling his situation.

And so, soon after my lifestorm that left me in such pain and confusion there was nowhere on this earth I could go for what

I needed, like most believers when suffering strikes, I went to the book of Job. Job made it safe for me to be brutally honest with my questions. But actually, I started at the back of the book: Job came to me first when I went back to the cemetery for the first time after the burial, and because God did a wondrous thing for me that day I said aloud in my car on the way back to Dallas, "God, I think I know what Job meant when he said his ears had heard of you, but now his eyes had seen you. Because, God, I saw you at that grave today in a way I have never seen you before."

The months since the funeral in Comanche, Texas, where Creath and I had grown up, had been difficult, and I had not been back to the grave since the burial. Although we had not lived there in twenty-seven years, our roots and our families were there, and we had been married there. We were two of those people of whom you could truly say, "You can take the kid out of the country, but you can't take the country out of the kid." We spent a great deal of time back home and eventually acquired a bit of ranchland where we built fence, carried rocks out of the fields, planted wheat, raised a few cattle, and hunted deer and turkey. We raised our kids with one foot in the city and one in the country—and the country "took" real well with them too. So going back without Creath was not something I wanted to do.

The old community cemetery where Creath is buried was a place where he and I had often walked when we went back home. As we strolled through the quiet setting we would talk of our lives, our children, and our dreams. It was a peaceful and comfortable place for us, a reflective place where we would sometimes stop by the graves of friends and family members and remember how they had touched our lives.

We always ended up sitting at the graves of my grandfather and my father, and Creath would tell me again what I already knew: that before he really even knew me, my grandfather had believed in Creath when he was much too young to be preaching in the country church where my grandfather was a loved and respected deacon. We would also talk of my father, who died of a massive heart attack in 1975 when he was just sixty years old, and I would tell Creath again what I had told him many times before, that my father taught me the meaning of unconditional love and that I missed him terribly even after all the years.

We would also stop at the gravesite where we knew we would one day be buried, and there we would talk of how fleeting life is and of the urgency to remain faithful to God's call to walk with the people in the ministry God had given us and keep reminding them, and ourselves, that God is doing a work so great in his children that it will take two worlds for it all to be known.

These were never morbid times for us. They were times when we reaffirmed our own belief in the preciousness of life and relationships, when we felt at ever deeper levels, as we got older, the graciousness of God to give us dreams to talk about and grow into, a ministry we loved, and the delight of sharing life together.

This day, though, I was going back alone. Every inch of my body was aching from all the stress of the past months, and with every mile of the three-hour trip in relentless rain I had to fight the urge to turn around and go back home.

When I got to the cemetery, the rain had become a mist that engulfed me in its silence and mixed with my tears. To kneel in that cemetery and place a red rose on that grave was to face raw reality at its bitterest. I cried as I grasped the finality of my loss. I was—and would ever be—without the one whose love had made my life beautiful. The pain of going on without him seemed unbearable, and I begged God to hold on to me real tight because I could not hold on any longer myself.

After a while I felt a quietness begin to settle over me, and what happened next totally surprised me. I began to cry again, but this time the tears came as I realized that even deeper than the pain I felt at losing Creath was my gratitude that I had ever had him in the first place. I realized what a gift I had been given to have been allowed to share his life and his ministry. And I knew that no amount of pain or heartache could take away the richness of the life we had enjoyed together.

I, who had told God many times in the years we were married that I couldn't live without Creath and didn't intend to try, was now standing on his grave looking up in that misty sky and saying aloud, "God, you really are good!" I knew the revelation welling up from inside me was God whispering, "I am here. You don't have to do this alone."

Even so, the questions came. The sleepless nights. The cries of sadness and loneliness. The anxiety of "What now?" The feelings of being totally inadequate to handle all the responsibilities of family, home, job, ministry transition, finances, and my own life. It seemed that for every moment of light there were hours of darkness. I bounced between knowing God's grace and wondering where God was. I found myself thanking him one minute and the next asking him why he could not make things a little better.

Everything I had ever been taught, everything I had ever believed, was being severely tested. I wrestled with the issues of faith and trust, with God's sovereignty in a world where tragedy and illness and sin leave none untouched in the course of time, with his lovingkindness when the cries of hurting people fill the air. I asked God a lot of questions. I asked him "Why?" I asked him, "Why Creath? Why not me? Why would you take Creath, a teacher and discipler who was clearly speaking the truth of your magnificent purpose for your children?" I asked, "Why these four men? Why now, when they each were committed to touching the world with the hope of your grace and peace that they themselves had found?" The fact that somewhere in my church background I had been taught not to ask why did not keep the question from rising up from within me.

And I asked "What now?" questions, identity questions, "How do I go on?" questions. However big or small, magnanimous or trite, trusting or fearful, I asked them all. Over and over I asked them, maybe with different words and with more or less intensity, but I reminded him often that whatever I understood about my life before suddenly had changed, and I did not recognize much about this new life I was supposed to carry on.

There were more. No question was too sacred. "Is God truly sovereign?" I asked. "Does he ordain all that happens to us? What about the promises of God's watchful care over us? Just how is God 'a father to the fatherless, a defender of widows'?" (Ps. 68:5). These were no longer theological questions; they had become real-life questions—*my* real-life questions. And I did not just ask the questions; I struggled with them. They did not pass through my thinking and leave me with some conclusion born of my upbringing. They stripped me of all my preconceived ideas and forced me to start over with the most basic question of all—"Do I believe God is all he says he is?"

In reading the book of Job while inside the storm, I was comforted that Job could not simply settle for the long-accepted religious answers when they did not make sense with his experience. When the atrocities of his physical condition worsened and the taunting of his comforters seemed never-ending, he chose to take both his experience and his questions and argue them before God. Even in the midst of his pain and confusion and despair, even under the silence of heaven, Job never trifled with the hopelessness of shutting God out. For whatever he did not understand about what was happening to him and why God had let it happen, he still trusted God enough to say, "Though he slay me, yet will I hope in him" (Job 13:15). I so wanted to come to that place when I could proclaim Job's words with my heart and not just my tongue. And so, along with Job, I kept coming back again and again with my pain and my questions.

Somewhere along the way I realized I was no longer looking for answers to my questions; instead, I was looking for a renewed sense of God as I asked them. I found myself praying one day, "Lord, answer for me the questions you can, and with those you can't, please teach me more about yourself." At least I had come to understand that I was asking of an infinite God explanations that my finite mind could not handle were he to give them.

Job and I became journey-mates during those early months and years of my loss and grief. I sought both comfort and courage from him. I listened as he unloaded on God his anger at the unfairness of his situation and his bitterness at having to endure the taunts of his friends. I wept as he lamented the day he was born and despised the physical pain and emotional agony he had to endure.

With Job I cried out to God, "Where are you?" and with Job I also came to proclaim, "I know that my Redeemer lives, and that in the end he will stand upon the earth. And after my skin has been destroyed, yet in my flesh I will see God; I myself will see him with my own eyes—I, and not another. How my heart yearns within me!" (Job 19:25–27).

I wondered often as I pondered Job's unyielding search for answers to his suffering: if Job had not laid his traumas bare before God, would they have eventually festered and left Job with little more than a weak resignation to his fate? If left unexpressed, would they have hardened his heart from the possibility that God just might have a bigger plan than Job could see in the midst of the trial? Was it Job's emptying himself that kept the scales from forming over the eyes of his heart so that when God called to him out of the whirlwind he could bow before God as the awesome, mighty Creator of the universe and know that the answers he sought were inconsequential to the majesty of God? Was it this sense of majesty that caused him to give voice to the words, "My ears had heard of you but now my eyes have seen you" (Job 42:5)?

God's thundering queries out of the whirlwind were not for Job alone. Through the ages they have brought us modern-day

Jobs up short when our complaints are met, not with explanations of God's grand design, but with the revelation of God himself. It is not that God ignores the severity of the suffering but that he knows we need more than answers. Max Lucado summed up the experience like this:

> Out of the thunder, he speaks. Out of the sky, he speaks. For all of us who would put ditto marks under Job's questions and sign our names to it, he speaks. . . . Questions rush forth. They pour like sheets of rain out of the clouds. They splatter in the chambers of Job's heart with a wildness and a beauty and a terror that leave every Job who has ever lived drenched and speechless, watching the Master redefine who is who in the universe. . . . God's questions aren't intended to teach; they are intended to stun. They aren't intended to enlighten; they are intended to awaken. They aren't intended to stir the mind; they are intended to bend the knees.[1]

God spoke to Job and thus to us. So if God should choose to leave our questions unanswered, let us listen carefully to his silence—he is giving us himself!

"Lord, God Almighty,
Maker of heaven and earth."
How easily we say these words,
How quickly we forget their meaning.

You are the sovereign God of the universe.
You made all that is,
And all that is depends on you for every moment of existence.
Even me.

This means that you know.
You know the suffering,
*   you know the confusion,*
*   you also know the eternal plan.*

Job didn't.
I don't.
But you do.

So, Lord,
When the suffering is too great,
*   and the questions too big,*
*   and the answers too few,*
Send us away limping if you must,
*   but don't let us shut you out.*
                                        Amen

5
A Long and Painful Journey

How long, O LORD? Will you forget me forever?
How long will you hide your face from me?
How long must I wrestle with my thoughts
    and every day have sorrow in my heart?
How long will my enemy triumph over me?

Look on me and answer, O LORD my God.
    Give light to my eyes, or I will sleep in death;
my enemy will say, "I have overcome him,"
    and my foes will rejoice when I fall.

But I trust in your unfailing love;
    my heart rejoices in your salvation.
I will sing to the LORD,
    for he has been good to me.

Psalm 13

*I lived in the Psalms. I was certain, because of the Psalms, that I could trust
God with the full range of my human emotions. What I did not know was
that this trust is a daily decision and is not a secure possession to be taken
for granted.*

Randy Becton
*Does God Care When
We Suffer?*

One year. Such a minuscule bit of time in eternity," I found myself writing in a newsletter at the one-year mark on my journey of grief. "But how very long when the days are uncertain and the nights are so lonely. The passing of time allows some routine back into daily life, but it does not seem to ease the pain. A hundred hurts flood in at a memory, a glance at Creath's picture, or the sound of his name, and I cry at the unbearable thought of life without him."

I wanted to feel better. To not hurt so badly. To have already learned whatever it was I needed to learn. To finally have things be a little easier. "How long, O Lord, how long?" In a way one year seemed like such a short time, like it was only yesterday that I was quite happy with my life. In another way it seemed like a lifetime ago that happiness had filled my days.

Nothing had changed, and everything had changed. I lived in the same house, worked in the same profession, shopped in the same places, saw the same people, was surrounded by the same loving family—yet nothing felt the same. A part of me died in that plane crash and nothing, however unchanged, had escaped the ravages of that rogue wind.

"How long must I wrestle with my thoughts and every day have sorrow in my heart?" the psalmist cried. And I wondered will this pain ever go away? Will I ever again think clearly? Will anything in the days to come hold any sense of contentment? Will you forget me forever, Lord, and let the enemy named Despair have the last word: "I have overcome her"?

Self-pity? Maybe. Reality? Yes. I daresay no one who stands in the debris of a lifestorm has not struggled with such feelings. Sadly, sometimes the uninitiated voices of the religious community rise up and ask, "Where is your faith?" and the suffering devout scamper for a place to hide. When the hurting Christian begins to fear the fine line between facing the reality of the pain and wallowing in self-pity, the pain too often gets stuffed into some room down inside and replaced with glowing rhetoric.

Or, rather than deny the pain, anger at the unfairness replaces the self-pity.

But would not the psalmist have us cry out in our anguish and reach upward with a weak and uncertain hand? Would not he say to us that God hears such pleas offered in the desperation of knowing we cannot heal ourselves? Would he not tell us that the way to trusting in God's unfailing love is through the valley of shadow and death and pain and confusion and dread and fear—and in finding that, indeed, he goes ahead of us and positions himself along the way to take the load from us, one hurt at a time?

I am convinced that there is no healing without an honest confrontation of the myriad of feelings that blow in with the storms of life. Grief, from whatever source, is a long and painful journey. And, I found, it is full of frightful choices. The urge to retreat into a cocoon-like existence is great, and depression is slipped into so easily. The allure of escaping into busyness or pleasurable fancies also raises its ugly head.

Alongside all of this temptation that would take us further and further from healing lies the sometimes obscure choice of acceptance. Obscure because this path leads into the pain and makes no promise of a quick cure. Instead, it opens the wound to its very depth and applies the healing balm of God's very special grace from the inside out.

Will I sound like one who has no faith if I use the words *empty, alone, weary, frightened, inadequate,* or *lonely* to describe the feelings I lived with every waking moment of every day for many, many months? I could list more: *insecure, guilty, tired, overwhelmed, angry, doubtful, painful.* Echoing down through page after page of my journals from the early days of this journey are the sounds of immense heartache and the musings of one who had to struggle with feelings of despair in spite of all the promises of Scripture. Sometimes I wondered if those promises were meant for someone else. But I also found there, alongside the words of heartache, words such as *grateful, joy, anticipation, blessings, goodness, love, miracle, peace, acceptance, trust, hope.*

I found myself saying to my grown children late one night as we all lay across my bed talking about feelings "You know, kids, if I ever doubted the goodness of God before, I know it now to be a certainty."

I knew I did not understand the *why* of tragedy, but neither did I understand the touches of love and caring that were getting me through the days. In the valley and at points along the way, God gave me a hug here, a word of encouragement there, a little light in a very dark stretch of road, a glimpse of eternity, a reason for hope—but nowhere did he show me a shortcut through the valley. He simply kept leading me along and re-minding me, as I was able to hear it, that no matter how alone I felt, I was not alone.

We all become myopic in pain. Our vision is narrowed to the immediate, and all our energy goes just to surviving the next few minutes. Sometimes the pain takes up all of our in-sides, and there is no room to feel any other presence, even if it is divine. C. S. Lewis wrote,

> You can't see anything properly while your eyes are blurred with tears. You can't, in most things, get what you want if you want it too desperately: anyway, you can't get the best out of it. . . . And so, perhaps with God. I have gradually been coming to feel that the door is no longer shut and bolted. Was it my own frantic need that slammed it in my face? The time when there is nothing at all in your soul except a cry for help may be just the time when God can't give it: you are like the drowning man who can't be helped because he clutches and grabs. Perhaps your own reiterated cries deafen you to the voice you hoped to hear. . . . After all, you must have a capacity to receive, or even omnipotence can't give. Perhaps your own

> passion temporarily destroys the capacity. . . . Aren't all these notes the senseless writhings of a man who won't accept the fact that there is nothing we can do with suffering except to suffer it?[1]

Lewis also wrote, "Suffering is not good in itself. What is good in any painful experience is, for the sufferer, his submission to the will of God."[2] Do I ever submit to the will of God the questions I do not ask, the fears and doubts I refuse to acknowledge? Is it only as I take the feelings that threaten to destroy me emotionally, those that force my faith into a position of closer scrutiny, and look at them without dressing them up that I can then lay them at the feet of the Lord for his grace and healing? Even Christ struggled with the suffering that lay ahead before he relinquished himself to the Father's will. In the Garden of Gethsemane, we are told, he agonized in prayer until his sweat was as drops of blood. Three times he fell on the ground before the Father, "overwhelmed with sorrow to the point of death" (Matt. 26:38). And before he prayed, "Yet not as I will, but as you will," he prayed, "My Father, if it is possible, may this cup be taken from me" (Matt. 26:39). The word we find translated "yet" or "nevertheless" would indicate that a battle was going on, a confrontation with feelings that demanded attention before they could be submitted to a will higher than his desire to be freed from the suffering.

My friend Randy Becton "lived in the Psalms," as he said, able to trust God with the full range of his emotions. A young minister, husband, and father, Randy struggled to reconcile his theological understanding of suffering under the banner of a good God as he watched his mother's battle with cancer and then was himself diagnosed with the dread disease. Surgery and chemotherapy brought a remission of the cancer, and again life held great promise. But seven years later Randy was back in Houston with a new malignancy that would require him to be hospitalized for treatments one week out of every three for an entire year.

Randy has felt and explored the gamut of emotions that are inherent in any lifestorm. He talks of fear, of loneliness that feels cosmic, of helplessness and the horrors of illness, confusion, and depression, and he explores questions of God's love and of his silence. Cancer-free for twelve years now, Randy understands the long and painful journey of lifestorms, and because he has learned to say with Job, "Though he slay me, yet will I hope in him" (Job 13:15), he is able to hold out a hand of caring, give a touch of love, and speak a word of encouragement for all those God brings his way, as he has done so many times with me. Randy and his wife, Camilla, and I have often talked about our common experiences of having to deal with the rawness of an open wound and finding that, in exposing the wound to the light, the healing balm of God's grace could do its deepest work.

The way of healing is rarely painless and rarely quick. Perhaps I am a slow learner, but it seems that whatever happens to me I have to wrestle with all the way to my toes. I do not let go easily of either pain or pleasure. I often ask the same question of both: "Why?" I look at each from the inside, the outside, the upside, and the downside.

Perhaps I am a little too reflective for my own comfort, but this I know: When I wrestle with an issue in my life, when I allow myself to feel whatever is going on inside me, think about whatever I feel and refuse to let it go until I can sigh as I think of it rather than moan, or when I can accept that it can only rest in the hands of God—when I reach that place, however long it may take, I know that that experience, whether pain or pleasure, has become a part of who I am and I am the richer for it.

And so, long and painful though it has been, I am grateful that along the way I somehow keep finding the voice to say, "But, I trust in your unfailing love."

Father. O Father.

Sometimes the cries of anguish
rising up from the depths of our wounded hearts
drown out your whispers of comfort.

And we wonder why you can't speak as loudly
as the voices that would rob us of all hope.

At times it seems as if this will be forever,
Like the pain will never go away
and we will be doomed to living the rest of our lives
simply trying to survive.

Healing is so slow.

We would prefer a quick cure,
or at least a strong anesthetic to mask the pain.

We are tempted to ask you just
to let us forget what it is we are struggling with,
whatever has brought on this torment in our souls.

We don't want to think, to feel, to cry anymore.

But, Lord,
You have a better plan.

You would use these dark days
to teach us more about ourselves,
more about life,
more about you.

Help us to not turn away
and try to find an easier route.

Help us to trust in your unfailing love.

*Bring the healing balm of your grace into our sorrow
and make us whole again.*
Amen

6
Do You Want to Get Well?

I have set before you life and death, blessings and curses. Now choose life, so that you and your children may live and that you may love the LORD your God, listen to his voice, and hold fast to him. For the LORD is your life.

Deuteronomy
30:19–20

Our chance to be healed comes when the waters of our own life are disturbed. We can plunge into them and emerge new, or we can sit there by the churning depths of our inner world, justifying our existence as it is.

Elizabeth O'Conner
Search for Silence

There was a pool named Bethesda in old Jerusalem, a pool that on occasion was disturbed by a bubbling of the waters. Legend had it that an angel would come and stir the waters, and the first person to get into the pool after the angel's visit would be healed.

As you might imagine, the colonnades around the pool were crowded with the lame, the infirm, the blind, the paralyzed. No doubt most of them were brought there day after day by relatives or friends and left to while away the time with the others as they waited for the stirring of the waters.

Then one day, not an angel, but the Lord himself walked among the suffering masses there. He approached a man who had been an invalid for thirty-eight years. Jesus knew he had been in this condition for a long time, and he asked him, quite simply, "Do you want to get well?"[1]

I am struck with how much of myself I see in the man's reply. He did not immediately, with tearful expectation, strain forward and say with equal simplicity, "Yes, I do!" No, he began to give excuses why he was not well. "I have no one to help me into the pool when the water is stirred," he said. "While I am trying to get in, someone else goes ahead of me." And I wonder if he wasn't also thinking, *So, what chance do I have?*

The question, "Do you want to get well?" does not ask for an explanation; it calls for a heart response. Simple, or so it would seem. Who wouldn't want to get well? But what we, in the age of therapy, have come to know is that being in need of healing is not limited to the physically infirm. When we are ill or physically impaired we are quick to find every medical means possible to help us get well. No doubt our answer to the question would be a straightforward "Yes!" But when we are in emotional despair, we often come to believe that life will never be any different, and the will to live becomes a weak shrug of the shoulders. Hope is lost in the heart, not in the body.

I encountered the question over and over again in my own life. I heard it every time I found myself having to go some-where alone, make a decision that was way over my head, or do something well outside my comfort zone—anytime I was tempted to lock myself in my house behind closed shutters. I heard it when I felt the cold emptiness of a future looming ahead of me without the one I thought would be there to grow old with me. I heard it loudly and clearly whenever one of my children, on the other end of the phone, asked again, "Mom, will you be all right?" I heard it when I would sit down with a pen and a yellow pad to write a newsletter to the ministry fellow-ship that had been part of our life together, knowing that others were wondering, too, if I would be all right. I was wondering the same thing.

So I came to feel some empathy for the man who had lived a lifetime with whatever made him an invalid. It is probably a safe guess that he was not in a great deal of physical pain and that he had learned how to live life by depending on someone else to meet his needs. He knew who he was on that porch with the others who could not do for themselves. If he were well, who would he be? What would be expected of him? What would the others waiting by that pool think? What was the world like for one who must assume responsibility for himself? Who would his friends be? Could he make it as a healthy, responsible member of society? He had not had to face any of these questions in thirty-eight years. No wonder he hedged when asked if he wanted to get well.

And I, too, hedged. For a very long time, I hedged. For more than twenty-seven years, my identity, quite happily, was tied up in being the wife of a beloved minister. To be the person, the wife, that he needed me to be was the desire of my life. I saw this in no way lessening my commitment to God; I saw it as God's assignment for my life, one I gladly accepted. I loved Creath completely and found great contentment in his happiness.

We had had enough years together to work through the raw edges and rough places in our relationship and had become very comfortable with each other, as best friends always do. Now here I was, clutching my new identity as his widow, lying beside my pool of Bethesda with the Lord standing in front of me asking, "Do you want to get well?" I was not answering the question any better than the man confronted in Scripture.

I can remember asking myself during those days when we did not know the fate of the long-overdue plane, *Is there a me without Creath?* Later I would find myself standing in front of a mirror and asking, *Who, in heaven's name, are you?* and the even more disturbing question, *Who do you want to be?*

I wondered if the friendships we had enjoyed together would remain mine without him. I wondered if I would make

new friends. I shuddered at the thought of even looking at a
calendar and making any kind of plans without him.

Do you want to get well? The question was too much for me,
and all I could answer was, *Not at the moment.*

As time went on and the sun kept coming up in the
morning and I knew I was going to survive, the question took
on a new twist: *If I get well, how will people relate to me? When
I am no longer the grieving widow, will we have anything to talk
about? When I am better and can walk again, will they still want
to see me? Was the man by the pool who gave his excuse of not
being well as scared as I am now?*

The question of whether I *wanted* to get well took quite a
long time to settle. The question of whether I *would* get well, no
matter what it required or how long it took, was answered
quickly in an encounter with my youngest child.

One morning several weeks after the accident I woke up
early, as I always did, and literally pulled the covers up over my
head. I wondered why on earth I was going to bother with getting up. But, as I always did, in five minutes I was on the floor
and starting my day in the fog I had become accustomed to.

A little later when my college-age son and daughter were
in the kitchen with me I must have made some reference to
wondering why I even got up—I honestly do not remember
what I said. I had been so careful to not make my children feel
as if they were less important to me than their dad, but I had
also tried to help them understand that since the day they
were born I began preparing to give them up, to turn them
loose to follow their own lives. Not so with their dad. But
whatever I said that morning prompted a response from
Stephen later that day. That afternoon he and some friends were
leaving to go do something together, and I walked outside with
them to see them off. As the others were getting in the car,
Stephen turned around and came back to me. He put his arms
around me, gave me a hug, and said, "Mom, I have a reason for
you to get up in the morning." I innocently asked him what,

and, with tears in his eyes, he simply pointed to himself and said, "I love you."

I knew at that moment, that split second, that I would get well. I knew I owed it to our children to test and prove in the valley that the faith their dad and I, and they themselves, professed was to be believed, especially when life doesn't make sense. I knew that when I was ready to give up, the faces of my three children would keep me going.

I began praying that God would help me do much more than just survive this loss, that he would help me really learn to live a new life with joy and contentment in his steadfast love so that if they should ever lose a spouse or a child they would know that they could make it through that storm too.

That happened in the summer of 1987, a few weeks after the plane crash. It took more than two years before I began to feel that I was really on my way to getting well. A few days after New Year's Day, 1990, I woke up to the realization that my feelings were changing—quite literally I woke up to a song that helped me put my thoughts and feelings into words, first in my journal that morning, then into the ministry newsletter. I tried to rewrite it for this book but decided I couldn't say it any better than I had from that New Year's Day vantage point.

Early this morning as my clock-radio came on I heard the familiar voices of the Bill Gaither Trio singing a song that Bill and Gloria Gaither, along with Chris Christian, had written, called "Then Came the Morning."[2]

The song tells of the confusion and pain that Mary, the disciples, and other followers of Jesus felt as they watched the crucifixion. But something deep inside of them kept hearing him say that he would live again. Just when all looked the bleakest, the song says, "Then came the morning; night turned into day; the stone was rolled away; hope rose with the dawn. Then came the morning; shadows vanished with the sun;"—then the words that caused me to sit up with a start, as if they had been written for me this very morning—"Death had lost, and life had won; for morning had come."

Death had held me in its grip for two and a half years. The airplane crash that took Creath from me also took my desire to live. I had asked the Lord for many years to take me when he took Creath, and for most of these months past I could only think of how it would be to join him in the realms of heaven.

But the Lord had other plans, and I tried very hard to pray that his will, not mine, be done. Sometime in those early weeks after the accident I read the words in Psalm 27 that both promised and admonished:

I am still confident of this:
>   I will see the goodness of the Lord
>   in the land of the living.
Wait for the Lord;
>   be strong and take heart
>   and wait for the Lord. (vv. 13–14)

I remember thinking, *Okay, Lord. I haven't the slightest idea how you plan to pull this one off. But I'll believe it, and I'll try to hold on until you can show it.*

As I became more open to his way, I saw many goodnesses of the Lord—blessings that could only come from his hands—but the shadow of death was still with me. Two years into the valley I began to wonder if, indeed, life would always hurt so bad. I often found myself praying, "I believe. Help thou mine unbelief," and saying "Lord, I don't want to go on. But I want to want to."

As I look back now on my waiting on the Lord, I know that even though I didn't feel the sunshine above the clouds, somehow I believed the sun was there; even though I didn't feel open to life, I wanted to. Even though I didn't always *feel* God's presence, I *knew* it. I remembered Creath's saying many times that with God, the best is always yet to be. And that was the hope that anchored my soul in those days when life seemed so gray.

A few weeks ago I found myself in a place I did not want to be with a task I did not want to do, thinking thoughts I did not want to think. I was as close to being angry as I have ever been during this journey, and I wrestled with the Lord over some feelings I was more than ready to get rid of. I finally said, "Lord, whether I am here by your design to face some things I need to deal with, or I am here because of some choices of my own, the fact is, I'm here. And all I know to do now is keep taking the next step."

Then came the morning!

Those steps led me through some difficult decisions—and into a joyful surprise. On New Year's Day 1990, as I stood in my kitchen cooking the traditional steak and black-eyed peas, I suddenly realized I felt different inside. The sunshine I had believed in had broken through the clouds and flooded me with the assurance that I was seeing "the goodness of the Lord in the land of the living." I knew, as if by some revelation, that I was coming to allow Creath his rightful place in my life. The love and richness we had shared could never be taken away from me, but no longer did he have to be the center of my life and emotions. It was as if I heard the Lord saying to me,

"I have set before you life and death, blessings and curses. Now choose life, so that you and your children may live and that you may love the LORD your God, listen to his voice, and hold fast to him. For the LORD is your life" (Deut. 30:19–20).

I do not write this without tears. And I do not know what other heartaches the Lord will allow to come my way. But this I know:

Death has lost, and life has won.
Morning has come.

O Father,
How do we thank you for your incomparable grace,
Grace that lets us hedge and avoid a direct answer
     when we simply cannot at the moment face the issue.
And yet, grace that will not leave us there,
     but will in time tell us to take up our bed and walk,
Because until our feet start moving
     we make no progress toward getting well.

It's not always easy to choose life, Lord
Because then we have to struggle with who we are
     and why we are, and who you are
And what to do with who we are,
     and why we are, and who you are.

We have to let you make us new,
     and being made anything always hurts.

But Lord,
The eyes watching to see if we will get well
     are eyes too precious to cloud over with our fear
          or anger,
               or doubt,
                    or our multiple excuses for not getting well.

Father,
Let morning come in our hearts,
So morning can come in our lives,
     And the world that needs a word of hope can hear
          "Death has lost, and life has won."
                         Amen

7

I Believe . . . Help Thou Mine Unbelief

[Thomas] said to them, "Unless I see the nail marks in his hands and put my finger where the nails were, and put my hand into his side, I will not believe it." . . .

Then [Jesus] said to Thomas, "Put your finger here; see my hands. Reach out your hand and put it into my side. Stop doubting and believe."

Thomas said to him, "My Lord and my God!"

John 20:25–27

The struggle to believe is possibly the mightiest conflict known to the soul of man. Faith does not always come from quiet contemplation or meditation. It is sometimes born among the raging of questions with no answers, pain with no relief, hope that has no reason to exist.

Glenn Owen,
foreword, *The Gift of Life* by Randy
Becton)

I believed and I doubted. I questioned and I embraced. I felt unbearable pain and unbounded joy. How can such opposites reside in the same space? Or are they truly opposites? Does one call forth the other? Can I believe as deeply if I have never doubted? Can I embrace as fully if I have never questioned?

Can I feel joy I can't explain if I have never felt pain that darkened my days?

How could I share anything with a word of certainty when I felt so uncertain myself? I knew much more with my head than my hurting heart could concur with, leaving me more than a little baffled. So when I was called by the teacher of a rather large young couples' Sunday school class at my church, I was quite prepared to say no. I was tired, I was emotionally drained, and I just didn't have the energy to tell the story one more time.

But before the word could come out of my mouth, I was given the topic: "Does God Keep His Promises?" I hung up the phone and answered aloud in the silence of my house, "Yes! And no." Then I asked with an upward glance, "Well, do you?" At that time I thought God must be as tired as I was because I wasn't hearing much from him.

Before my lifestorm I could have worked up a lovely devotional on God's promises and given good reasons why we should not doubt them. But God's promises were no longer devotional material; they were real-life issues. I knew I could not go to that class and tell those who gathered there how God keeps his promises, but I could assure them I was learning that he does. Even as I questioned his promises because of the pain that wouldn't go away, I knew I was learning that the problem is not with God's promises but with our bringing twentieth-century expectations and personal wish-fulfillment to those promises. The problem lies with our expectations of what God should do and how he should do it when life hurts. I was learning that I had to quit just looking at the promises of God and look to the God of the promises.

"Doubtstorms," Max Lucado calls them. "Turbulent days when the enemy is too big, the task too great, the future too bleak, and the answers too few."[1] He talks of those whose Bible hero is Thomas, and he poses tough questions, "throw-in-the-towel questions." He queries:

> "If God is so good, why do I sometimes feel so bad?"
> "If his message is so clear, why do I get so confused?"
> "If the Father is in control, why do good people have gut-wrenching problems?"
>
> You wonder if it is a blessing or a curse to have a mind that never rests. But you would rather be a cynic than a hypocrite, so you continue to pray with one eye open and wonder:
>
> —about starving children
> —about the power of prayer
> —about the depths of grace
> —about Christians in cancer wards
> —about who you are to ask such questions
>   anyway.[2]

I do not remember a time when I did not believe in God. I was raised in a home and an extended family that held the basic tenets of the Christian faith as sacred. I never questioned them. I married a minister when I was quite young and continued on in my absolute belief in God as the creator and sustainer of all life, in Jesus Christ as the very Word of God who came to live among us and die for us, and in the Holy Spirit as our teacher and guide (although my particular tradition didn't talk much about the Holy Spirit, seemingly concerned that someone might get a little carried away).

My faith was not a side issue in my life; it was the very center of my whole existence. I always felt quite certain about the "big picture" of faith, and I loved all the religion classes I took in college and the Bible studies and hundreds of sermons I learned from. Even so, as an adult married to a minister, much of my confidence in the faith I professed was actually my confidence in Creath. I so trusted his walk with the Lord and his understanding of God's ways with humanity that I deferred to him any question that might come to the surface with me. He did not take the place of God in my life, but he was my greatest teacher, and I was only too happy to let *him* wrestle with what I believed.

Then the day came when he was no longer there. The questions, the fears, the doubts, the ways of God with humanity were now mine to wrestle with, alone. Again and again I would read in Scripture the story of the father who, more than anything, wanted his child to be free from the evil spirit that threatened his life. With great empathy I would read the words, "I believe; help thou mine unbelief."[3] I felt that maybe this father would understand if he heard me say, "Lord, it's not that I don't believe that you are who you said you are and that you can perform miracles; it's just that I don't know how you are going to handle this particular situation and how I will survive if you do something other than what I am asking." Maybe it's that my belief was stronger than my faith. The actual translation from the Greek says it for me: "I am believing. Be helping my weakness of faith."

The tension between faith and doubt is staggering to a reflective personality like myself. The tension for me is not between believing and not believing but in deciding what to believe about the things that are subject to interpretation.

When I read C. S. Lewis' *A Grief Observed* after the accident, it said some very different things to me than when I had read it some years before. I even sat down at the typewriter and copied three pages of quotes from the book and realized that I could chart my own grief journey by that of Lewis. He said some very strong things, and I could understand why, when it was first published, the religious publisher would not use his real name as author because the publisher was afraid it would create great anxiety among the religionists of that day. And yet, I wonder if a faith we are afraid to examine with the harshest of judgment is strong enough to withstand the crisis of great suffering.

Lewis said, "You never know how much you really believe anything until its truth or falsehood becomes a matter of life and death to you."[4] In the book Lewis struggled openly with those places where the faith he professed didn't match up to the pain he was feeling. He struggled with what he believed about God, at one point crying, "Not that I am (I think) in much danger of ceasing to believe in God. The real danger is of coming to believe such dreadful things about him."[5] He risked examining his faith closely to determine if what he believed was true or if it was a faith of his own making. He surmised, "If my house has collapsed at one blow, that is because it was a house of cards."[6]

As I read over and over again the cries from Lewis's dark night of the soul and felt acutely my own, I also read again and again the rest of his story and his musings after a little healing had taken place: "My idea of God is not a divine idea. It has to be shattered time after time. He shatters it Himself. . . . Could we not almost say that this shattering is one of the marks of His presence? . . . I mustn't sit down content with the phantasmagoria itself and worship that for Him. Not my idea of God, but God."[7]

I think perhaps in all my doubting, in all my cries of "I believe; help thou mine unbelief" (and there were many such cries), I was seeing the shattering of my false ideas of God and the coming into being of a trust that did not depend on my understanding. I no longer feared the "raging of questions with no answers" but wrote endlessly about them in my journals.

I allowed myself to question God as I left a dinner party one evening where someone who knew nothing of my particular loss had talked extensively about how he and his family survived a near-fatal airplane crash. Driving home alone because of another airplane crash—one that *was* fatal—I cried aloud, "How did you make the choice to save that family and take our husbands? Couldn't you as easily have saved them both?"

I could sit in a chair when the constant emotional pain had sapped so much of my energy that I had no physical strength to do anything and ask God if he was, indeed, close to the broken-hearted and if he did, indeed, save the crushed in spirit as the psalmist said. And if so, then why was I still brokenhearted and crushed? Since I was now a widow and my children were fatherless, I could ask him just how, practically speaking, he was a father to the fatherless and a friend of widows.

As I would ponder these questions and countless others like them, I would hear the plaintive whisper rising up from within me, "I really do believe. Please help me to believe more and more in spite of the questions with no answers."

I found that I embraced the questions. I discovered that, rather than creating more doubt they were raising up faith. Rather than turning me away from God, they were drawing me toward him. Rather than making me angry when what I seemed to be reading in Scripture didn't match my immediate experience, I was challenged to read more and try to see a picture bigger than the eight-by-ten glossy of my pain.

Scripture tells us that God's ways are not our ways and his thoughts are higher than our thoughts. In Jesus' last discourse to his disciples he finally said to them, in essence, "There are so many more things I have to tell you, but you can't handle them now."

As I struggled to leave with God the mystery of why life must sometimes hurt so badly, I thought back to a time when Stephen, then almost three years old, must have been torn between trusting me to protect him and wondering why I was letting the doctor hurt him. It was a very painful experience for this mother, as it would be for any parent, but it taught me something about trusting beyond what we can understand. Stephen had to have two corrective surgeries, and in between he had to have frequent checkups that often required a procedure that was simple but painful for him. This all began when Stephen was young enough not to suspect what was happening until it was almost over. But as he grew older, he began to anticipate what the doctor might do, and he built up a great deal of resistance once we got into the doctor's office.

On one particular occasion when the doctor needed to clip some tissue, Stephen began to grab for me and try to get off the table, crying and begging, "Please don't let him cut me!"

I knew if I fell apart they would make me leave the room, and I wasn't about to leave him in there without me, so I leaned across him and choked back the tears as I tried to reassure him it would be over soon. There was no way I could insist that we just skip the procedure and stop the pain. Nor could I explain to Stephen's little three-year-old mind why this had to be done. All he knew was that the doctor was going to cut him and it was going to hurt.

And yet, with all his screaming and crying he clung to me—he knew I would be there when it was all over. I held my own screaming and crying inside for many days, because everyday living had to be attended to—but when the tears came, I was glad I was alone!

I have since reflected on this many times, and I wonder if God doesn't also shed tears when he sees us, his children, hurting badly and he knows our finite minds simply could not understand even if he explained to us why it must be so. Instead he just whispers to us, "Trust me. I am here. I can see what you can't."

These last years have been an incredible journey of belief and doubt, trust and fear, raging questions and simple faith. And the journey goes on. Perhaps because I have asked so many questions and sought so many answers, I have at least come to know enough about God that when I doubt his love, I hold to his wisdom. When I can't understand his justice, I cling to his mercies. When I wonder about his faithfulness, I cherish his grace. When I fear his sovereignty, I bow to his holiness. And in that my heart can rest.

Lord, believing isn't easy
   when I'm hurting,
      or confused,
         and you are silent for so long.

And when I do believe,
   it's most often not with all of me.

Like Thomas,
I have to be shown over and over again,
   not only the wounds in your hands and side,
   but proof that you love me.

O, divine Lord,
Help me to look beyond my wishes for peace and comfort,
   beyond my doubts and unanswered questions,
      to the tear in your eye
         as you carry the pain
            too heavy for me to bear.
                           Amen

8
The Greater Miracle

But they that wait upon the LORD shall renew their strength;
they shall mount up with wings as eagles; they shall run, and
not be weary; and they shall walk, and not faint.

Isaiah 40:31 KJV

I realize there are people who tell you that religion can make
everything easy and who claim that any time a person prays,
he is caught up in light and soars above his problems until they
appear small and inconsequential. But I don't believe such
words! There are moments in the depths of human suffering
when the soaring of ecstasy would be out of touch with reality.

John Claypool
Tracks of a Fellow
Struggler

Miracle. Has a nice ring to it, doesn't it? Most of us have experienced one or two, whether or not we recognized—or admitted—it. There have been those times, either for us or for someone we know, when no explanation can suffice for the healing that even the doctors say should never have been, the event that by all practical reasoning should never have come together as it did, the "chance" meeting that developed into a relationship that neither could have ever planned, the birth of a precious baby after years of being told it could never be, the unexpected touch of kindness that got us through a seemingly impossible place. However grand and glorious or small and unnoticed by anyone else, it had to be a miracle.

We have surely experienced many more miracles that we hesitate to identify with that word because it seems to have taken a lot of work on *our* part to make these things happen! These are the things we could and should do something about. For example, the loss of material comforts due to a weakened economy can move us to find a serenity we had not known before as we learn to simplify our lives, even if we have no choice about doing so. A clinical depression can prompt us to seek help in dealing with the foes of our emotional stability and lead us to healthier ways of living and relating. Losing a job we had performed well for many years can allow us to un- cover gifts and talents we did not know we had as we apply ourselves to whatever opportunities may be there for us instead of waiting for the perfect situation. In coming to accept that the birth of a baby is not ours to experience we can choose to go through the arduous process of adoption and finally have that chosen child placed in our empty arms. The loss of some physical capacity can push us to develop other ways of per- forming, thus bringing to life a long-buried ability that enriches all who come our way. All of these accomplishments require an enormous amount of courage and perseverance, but could we truly have accomplished them in our own strength alone? Is not our transcendent spirit's surviving against all odds itself a miracle?

Then there are those times in life when there is nothing we can do to change the situation, nowhere we can go to get away from the loss, no one who can make things better. The darkness engulfing us makes it impossible to see a way out. All we can do is survive the empty moments as best we can and keep putting one foot in front of the other because we can do that auto- matically. Whether there will be a tomorrow is inconsequential; indeed, death often seems like a welcome end to the pain of liv- ing with the hole in our hearts, or with the guilt, or the shame, or whatever abyss the particular loss opened up. Then we look in vain for a miracle.

When life hurts we would like God to pick us up and let us soar above the heartache so that even though we know it is there we don't suffer the deep pain we might have anticipated. *Triumphant* is a word that rings clear. The silver lining on the clouds shines so brightly that the clouds are not so menacing. The pains of the trials take on the hue of dawn as life looks and feels much like all is well after all. This is what it means to "mount up with wings as eagles."[1] This is miracle at its best, we think.

If not such a triumphant miracle as this, then we would like God to at least keep us fully assured that the pain we are enduring will come to our desired end. We want to know he is on our side and working everything out for our good (preferably to our satisfaction). With the right inspiration we do not even mind working at the "miracle" ourselves, but we would like to see it unfolding to keep us adequately motivated, to allow us "to run and not grow weary."

Little do we know that the greater miracle in the midst of our most grievous storm is when God gives us what we need to simply "walk and not faint." At first glance this hardly seems like a miracle at all. But then we realize that soaring is out of the question, and there is no more running to be done. The only thing left is the helplessness of a reality that has forever changed the shape of life as we have known it and loved it. Now comes the "keep on keeping on" stage, when all we want is to go somewhere so we can coddle the gaping wound we have been left with and try to survive the unbearable pain. In the darkness of the tunnel, merely "keeping on" becomes a miracle. In his book, *Tracks of a Fellow Struggler,* John Claypool shared his own experiences of pain and miracles in the illness and death of his young daughter to leukemia. Reflecting on a relapse after a long remission, he related in a sermon he delivered to his congregation:

> I am sure that to those looking for the spectacular this
> may sound insignificant indeed. Who wants to be slowed

to a walk, to creep along inch by inch, just barely above the
threshold of consciousness and not fainting? That may not
sound like much of a religious experience, but believe me,
in the kind of darkness where I have been, it is the only
form of promise that fits the situation. When there is no
occasion to soar and no place to run, and all you can do
is trudge along step by step, to hear of a Help that will
enable you "to walk and not faint" is good news indeed.[2]

Ask the one who has just been handed divorce papers
when it seemed progress was being made in working through
the difficulties in the marriage. Ask the new mother looking
into the face of her baby she has just been told has Down's
syndrome. Ask the man nearing retirement age who has been
forced out of his position with no place to go. Ask the family
who is sorting through the charred ruins of their home, wondering how they will ever replace the necessities for living,
much less the memories that went up in smoke. Ask the one
whose diagnosis from the doctor leaves little hope for recovery.
Ask the ones sitting by the bedside as someone they love more
than life itself is drawing his or her last breath. Ask the one
who has just been told, "There has been an accident, and there are
no survivors." Ask these people if they were not thankful for
the grace to endure the blast that shocked both their bodies
and their spirits.

When the plane carrying my husband did not come home
that Sunday afternoon and there was no word through the
night, I knew the possibility existed that the plane would not
be found right away in the extensive mountain range they had
to cross. I hastily wrote down the words from Isaiah that promised, "He gives strength to the weary and increases the power
of the weak" (Isa. 40:29). Each day of that long week I carried
that piece of paper with me and pulled it out often to read again
the words I already knew so well.

I needed that promise then, and in the days that followed as I began traveling the road of widowhood. The tedious task of taking the next step often demanded more courage and strength than I could bring to the surface. At times I would pray, "Please, Lord. Just help me get through the next fifteen minutes." I did not dare pray for an hour, much less a day. And often I would find myself hunting a place to get away for a little while from the people around me so I could deal with the emotions that were threatening to undo me. Then I would have to pray, "Lord, we didn't do too well that time. Let's try for the next fifteen minutes."

When a storm comes along of sufficient force to wipe out our livelihood, our health, our most treasured relationship, or perhaps our lifelong dreams, and we are left standing in the rubble of our shattered lives, we are in many ways reduced to infancy. So much has been lost and so much changed that we must essentially start over again. We must begin to walk before we can think about running or soaring. Indeed, we need help just to be able to stay on our feet.

The thought of loss reducing us to infancy became clear for me when I was keeping my three-year-old granddaughter for several days. After I had just told her that I couldn't possibly pick her up one more time, Sara Beth held her arms up to me and said, "But, Grandmommy, I can't carry myself." I wondered how many times in my toddling through the last years I had said to God, "Please. I can't carry myself."

When we can't carry ourselves, when the loss is one we cannot rise above or work through but no amount of prayer or effort can restore, our most immediate need is the grace to survive the intensity of emotional despair and the physical fatigue that accompanies it. It is here that our faith is being sorely tested at the same time it sustains us. It is here that we often cry out from the depths of disillusionment, "Where are you, God?"

It is also here that God can do his deepest work in our lives because here we become aware that we have nowhere to go but to him.

And here . . .

> We can learn that trust does not depend on our understanding but on our willingness to believe when all the evidence of the moment asks, "Why should I?"

> We can pour out our screams of unfairness to God until we are empty enough for him to begin to teach us his absolute faithfulness.

> We can come to see God, ourselves, and our faith journey with new eyes as we simply hold out our hands and allow him to lead us into a greater awareness of his wisdom.

> We can allow him to teach us from the depths what we could never learn in the ecstasy of soaring or the exhilaration of running.

Truly, "to walk and not faint" may not only be the greater miracle, but it may well be our greatest discipler.

Lord, it is so dark down here in the depths.
We can't see you as clearly.

Or is it just the opposite?
Can you better show us yourself in all your glory
*   when there is less glitter?*
*   There is no glitter down here, Lord.*

We so long for the pain to be gone,
*   for the lessons to be learned,*
*   for the light to shine brightly again.*

Just as you give us the grace to walk in these impossible
    places in life,
so give us the grace to trust that we will again run,
    and even soar,
        as you bring healing to our wounds
            and wholeness to our faith.
                    Amen

9
Peace Not as the World

Peace I leave with you; my peace I give you. I do not give to you as the world gives. Do not let your hearts be troubled and do not be afraid.

John 14:27

Your solution to grief is just another way of giving the same answer that God gave me in the first empty days—accept this. Only in acceptance lies peace—not in forgetting nor in resignation nor in busy-ness.

Letter to Catherine Marshall from Elisabeth Elliot, quoted in *Beyond Ourselves*

Soon after the Vietnam War ended the American Art Institute opened a contest asking people to send their artistic rendition of the meaning of peace. The institute received hundreds of paintings, most of them the kinds of things that typically depict calmness and tranquility. Many paintings were of pastoral scenes with green valleys, quiet streams, and blue skies. Others were of people together in quiet settings and embraces. Still others were obviously personal and descriptive of some experience. In all, the responses were overwhelming in their portrayal of the kind of peacefulness we all desire.

However, in the painting the American Art Institute chose, the artist had captured a raging storm so vividly that, looking at it, you could almost hear the thunder. In the center of the picture was an open field, and there, nearly lost in the darkness of the clouds, the artist had painted a tree bowing to the strong winds. And in that tree was a nest where a mother bird hovered over her young. The one-word caption was simply: *Peace.*

That is the peace that "passes all understanding." It is peace in the midst of the storm, peace that comes with the cry, "Thy will, not mine, be done." Peace born of the assurance that we are not alone.

Peace is much less a condition than a state of mind. Anxiety and tension can rule the day even when the circumstances of my life would indicate that all should be well with me. I can walk in sunshine and see only the shadows. I can be surrounded by those I love and be consumed with fear of losing them. I can accomplish a great task and still wonder why I did not do better. Peaceful surroundings do not always make for a peaceful heart.

On the other hand, peace can be found in the strangest places. Corrie ten Boom in the German concentration camp. Elisabeth Elliott ministering to the very Auca Indians who had killed her husband. Joni Erikson Tada speaking a word of hope from her wheelchair. Friends I know who lost everything they owned in a business venture saying to me they wouldn't trade what they have learned about themselves, each other, and God, even if they could have it all back. And seeing the smile on my precious ninety-seven-year-old grandmother's face when she looked at us just hours before she died and said quietly, "I love you."

Peace, in the ultimate meaning of the word, is not the absence of conflict. It is not the accumulation of wealth, or comfort and ease, or a state of happiness. Peace is that sense down deep inside that says no matter what happens, all is well with my soul.

Not the kind of peace the world gives, Christ said. Not the kind that depends on circumstances but the kind that rests on the quiet confidence of trust in a loving, sovereign God. The kind that comes with the willingness to accept whatever life brings my way as an all-wise God's assignment to teach me more about who I am and who he is. It is the peace of an openness that invites him to use the events of my life to make me His servant.

"Only in acceptance lies peace," said Elisabeth Elliot, "not . . . in resignation."[1] Is there a difference in acceptance and resignation? Does one open the door to the peace that calms our troubled spirits when the pain of our losses seems more than we can bear and the other become a closed door on a windowless room? Is acceptance truly the only portal through which light can filter into the darkness and illuminate the possibilities of purpose and healing? Does resignation to the fact that there is nothing I can do to bring back what I have lost blind me to the miracles that grace can perform?

In a book called *Lord, If I Ever Needed You, It's Now!* that I helped my husband write as his resident grammarian, spell checker, editor, proofreader, and cheerleader, he gave this insight into acceptance and resignation in the healing and renewing process that comes with any major loss in our lives.

> Resignation is surrender to fate.
> Acceptance is surrender to God.
>
> Resignation lies down quietly in an empty universe.
> Acceptance rises up to meet the God who fills that universe
>   with purpose and destiny.
>
> Resignation says, "I can't."
> Acceptance says, "God can."
>
> Resignation paralyzes the life process.
> Acceptance releases the process for its greatest creativity.

Resignation says, "It's all over for me."
Acceptance asks, "Now that I am here, what's next, Lord?"

Resignation says, "What a waste."
Acceptance says, "In what redemptive way will you use this
    mess, Lord?"

Resignation says, "I am alone."
Acceptance says, "I belong to you, O God."[2]

When life has been permanently altered by some great crisis, all of us will sometimes feel, whether or not we actually say
the words, those attitudes that resignation brings up. Our ten-
dency is to clench our fists tightly around what was—as I did
because I could not imagine how tomorrow could hold any fulfillment at all without Creath. I wanted what I had had, not
what I could have. A part of me died in that airplane crash, and
I questioned how even God could fill the void left when there
was no Creath. As emptiness and pain and loneliness became
my constant companions, I was certain I would never again
know the contentment that once had been mine.

About eighteen months after the accident that catapulted me
into this journey, I found myself at an impasse. Even with the
wondrous things I had seen of God in the long days past, things
that left no doubt but that he was, indeed, a God who kept his
promises, I still carried immense sadness. My fists were indeed
tightly clenched around the life I had had with Creath, and I
was leaving God little, if any, room to even squeeze in a touch
of something new.

The job I had held as director of a program for children with
special learning needs in a private school was very demanding,
and the many months of taking care of more details of life than
I ever thought possible had all taken their toll. I knew I had to
get away and confront the despair that was threatening to over-
take me.

I went alone to a friend's farmhouse where I could cry without interruption, and I told God when I got there that I had no expectations of what he should do while I was there. I told him I was not going to make myself read the Bible or pray or think or anything else—I asked him to just let me rest awhile from all the pressures of this journey. And yet, as I walked through the pastures surrounding the farmhouse on those cold January days and sat in the evenings in front of a warm fire, I began to find myself talking to God as if he were a friend who had come along with me. I began reading Scripture with a hunger. And I read again *Tracks of a Fellow Struggler,* which became the catalyst for a turning point in my journey.

In the quiet of a cold, rainy afternoon I "listened" to John Claypool talk of how it was only when Job came face to face with the Creator God that he gained a new understanding of the past and a fresh vision of the future. Only then did Job realize that he still had a future in God; only then did he move from despair to hope.

What struck me then was that Job did not get back the same children or the same possessions or the same health as he had had before, as Claypool says, but what he did get back was a deepened and enlarged capacity for life. I was really "hearing" all of this when I turned to the last page of the book and read, "The One from whom had come 'the good old days' could be trusted to provide 'good new days.'"[3] I put the book down and thought about that for a while. Then I read the next sentence, actually a question: "If yesterday was so full of meaning, why not tomorrow?"[4] It was as if my tight fists began to unclench, and I wrote on the blank page at the end of the book:

> Was there meaning in my life solely because of Creath?
> Or was my life with Creath a wonderful bonus to the
> meaning in my life because of God? So does meaning

for me now become impossible because there is no Creath?
Or can there be renewed meaning because there is God?
I have lost Creath—I haven't lost God. One was a gift in
time; the other a gift for eternity.

I knew at that moment I had to stand before God with open
hands and accept whatever gifts he chose to give. And I knew
I could trust that there would be meaning in my tomorrows.

In the days that followed I went back to all the pressures
I had left behind, but I took a sense of release with me. I began
to feel some excitement about the possibilities of a "future in
God." To my surprise I began to see the sunshine and not just
the clouds. I knew, in a way I had not known before, an assurance that life would not always feel so bleak.

In that experience I learned the difference in acceptance
and resignation. I learned a peace that is certainly not of this
world, peace that comes with knowing God is working all
things for our good, no matter how much it may hurt. I learned
that God can fill only empty hands.

Lord,
I want to come to you with open hands,
but my heart keeps crying out for life the way I knew it.
So I'm afraid I have come to you with my fists tightly clenched,
        holding in the emptiness.
Help me to loosen my grip on what was,
        and bow before your goodness and your faithfulness.

Help me to trust that the meaning in the yesterdays of my life
        will surely be surpassed by the meaning in my tomorrows,
                because you are the source of all meaning.

And with you,
        the best is always yet to be.

Lord,
It would be so easy to shrug my shoulders in resignation
    and ask, "What's the use?"
And yet, O Lord,
I ask for grace to accept the losses in my life
    with full assurance that you are an all-wise, all-loving God
        who will grant peace and hope as I rest in you.
Your peace I desire in my inmost being.
Not the peacefulness of a painless life,
    but the calmness of a spirit
        that even in the midst of the storm can hear
            your gentle whisper,
        "Don't be afraid, my child, I am here."

O Lord,
Let me ever praise you with grateful heart,
    for you have dealt graciously with me,
        your fearful, needy child.
                        Amen

10
My Child . . .

The Lord your God is with you, he is mighty to save. He will take great delight in you, he will quiet you with his love, he will rejoice over you with singing.

Zephaniah 3:17

How can we but love Him when we know that He numbers the very hairs of our heads, marks our path, and orders our ways?

Charles Hadden
Spurgeon
Morning and Evening

I think that the last tear wiped away shall be a tear God brushes from his own eye."[1] I read this in a book called *A Tearful Celebration* in the first weeks after the lifestorm that left my world in complete disarray. It was what I needed to hear.

James Means wrote this book out of his struggles with the horrors of the cancer that took his wife from him and the perplexities of reconciling his faith with the realities of his suffering. He wrote, too, of the God who not only gives us strength for the present and hope for the future, but who shares in our pain.

As I read Means' description of his pain as an "intolerable burden of ten thousand bleeding wounds,"[2] I knew exactly what he was saying. Then I read, "In all of this personal odyssey of catastrophic events, there is this rising, absorbing thought: *God knows and feels our pain.*"[3] I read, "I feel that life has caved in and I am in some black mudhole."[4] And then, "God knows what best promotes His objectives. The darkness of this hour and the loneliness of this grief testify to the symphony of God's love for me. It is a symphony written in a minor key, but beautiful nonetheless."[5] In his writing his pain always had the companionship of a good and loving God.

In trying to make some sense out of what seemed a senseless tragedy, I needed to see God's sovereignty, his wisdom and power and grace. I needed also to see his love and his tenderness. I needed to see an omnipotent God who not only brings strength to counter my weakness, but who also weeps with me in my sorrow. James Means said for me things I knew I believed about God, but things that had been obscured for a time by the immensity of my pain. He took the veil off for me, and through his writing he helped me allow God to put his arms of comfort around me and whisper, "My child."

The most determinative thing about the way we live our lives and most certainly the way we walk through the valleys is what we, in the deepest part of our beings, believe God is like.

In his book *Disappointment With God,* Philip Yancey deals with three questions, "Is God unfair? Is God silent? Is God hidden?" He wrote, "What we think about God, and believe about God, matters—really matters—as much as anything in life matters."[6]

In *Does God Care When We Suffer?,* Randy Becton said, "In moments of anguish, the issue is more than our pain; it is our God . . . The knowledge of suffering's place in the scheme of things is God's to possess. That's why it is absolutely necessary that we know what kind of God we have."[7]

A.W. Tozer, in *The Knowledge of the Holy,* wrote, "What comes into our minds when we think of God is the most important thing about us. . . . The most portentous fact about any man is not what he at a given moment may say or do, but what he in his deep heart conceives God to be like. . . . That our idea of

God corresponds as nearly as possible to the true being of God is of immense importance to us."[8]

As I moved further and further into my quest to know God beyond my perceptions of him formed out of a composite of my life experiences as much as out of an understanding of Scripture, I found that I was, and am, continually in danger of bringing God down in my thinking to my level of ability to comprehend. My mind expanded ever so slowly to let him be God beyond my understanding. I must confess that every new life experience still brings new questions and new doubts, but these same experiences also bring opportunity for deeper acceptance of the mystery that surrounds an infinite God whose thoughts and ways I cannot fathom with my finite mind.

In Isaiah the Lord declared, "As the heavens are higher than the earth, so are my ways higher than your ways and my thoughts than your thoughts" (Isa. 55:9). Rather than giving me reason to distrust him, this verse gives me the comfort of knowing that I am not left to one whose resources are no greater than my own.

I have found, as I am sure most of us have when we open our eyes and find only darkness, that what I want is not mystery, but assurance. I not only want to know that God is all-powerful and good and wise and loving, I want to *feel* it. I want his presence to be so real that the dark becomes light. I want answers to my questions of "Why?" and "What now?" and "Will all of this come out okay?"

I have also found that that is most often not the way he works. God is doing a greater work in us, and that can only come as we learn to trust him no matter how dark the days and sleepless the nights. And it is only as we have been through the darkness with him that what we know with our heads slides down into our hearts, and our hearts no longer demand answers. The Why? becomes unimportant when we believe that God can and will redeem the pain for our good and his glory.

This was true for me. It was in the darkness of my valley that my heart cried out for God to be too big for me to understand. I knew that if I could put him in a box and explain him to anyone who asked he wouldn't be big enough to get me through the unbearable pain and bring me to the place that life would again have meaning. So I continue to ask my questions, to struggle with some of the promises in Scripture that do not seem to match up with the sorrows of life. I still feel immense dismay at the senseless tragedies all around us, and I wonder at how the suffering of a child could be allowed by a perfect God. Even more, I continue to cling to what I do know: that he is a loving, sovereign God who is infinitely good and wise, one not bound by the human limitations I must live with.

When I put the sovereignty of God beside his unfailing love, my heart can rest.

I wonder if we don't need to go to God from time to time with the prayer that he would erase from our minds all of our preconceived ideas of him that he might give us a fresh glimpse of himself, not only in his sovereignty and power and wisdom, but in his love and faithfulness. There seems to be a real danger in our Christian culture that we major on right theology and miss altogether the simple beauty of his love. I have often thought how comforting it would be if I could really believe with the assurance of my four-year-old grandson that God loves me. This thought came to me one day when Will backed up to me so I could reach around and hug him as he said, "Grandmommy, you just love me so bad."

On one of those days when I felt great despair a friend read to me a little verse tucked away in Zephaniah (which itself is tucked away in the middle of the Old Testament), and I marveled at the thought of such love: "The Lord your God is with you, he is mighty to save. He will take great delight in you, he will quiet you with his love, he will rejoice over you with singing" (Zeph. 3:17).

If I could even begin to understand this kind of love, I might be able to understand more of his ways. But what I tend to do instead is say, "Are you talking to me?"

I find it very hard to let myself take in this kind of love. Yet over and over God is saying to us, in more ways than we can count, "I really do love you." Nothing could be more important for us to grasp or for us to tell one another. And nothing is more critical to the perspective we bring to our reading of all of Scripture than to believe that God really loves us.

I was in a retreat with Richard Foster where he was sharing about the writing of his book called simply, *Prayer*. He told us that at one point he had read so much about prayer and gathered so much material and delved so deeply into the subject that he was completely overwhelmed. He said he told the Lord he just couldn't do the book. Then as he struggled with his frustration at the enormous task, a peaceful quietness filled that library where he was working, and he felt as if he heard the Lord whispering, "Just tell my people that I love them."[9]

Just tell my people that I love them. What difference would it make in our lives if we really believed that with all our hearts; if we believed that God longs to give us himself and all his resources of love and goodness and wisdom? And what difference would it make if our deepest and most fervent prayer was that God would give us a love for him and his purpose that encompasses all we are and all we do?

God longs to give us himself. He longs to fill our lives with love when we don't feel lovable and grace when we can't take another step and peace when the storm is raging about us and joy when the tears of sadness are still on our faces. But we insist on running our own lives, choosing pleasure or comfort or security over the slower process of a changed life. And a changed life always involves pain; it always involves waiting; it always comes with the temptation to seek the easy way out.

A very long time ago I heard Creath say, "I am convinced that what grieves the heart of God the most is not the bad things we do, but the good that we miss. It is a plaintive voice that weeps, "'O Jerusalem, Jerusalem . . . How often I have wanted to gather your children together as a hen gathers her chicks beneath her wings, but you wouldn't let me'" (Matt. 23:37 TLB).

If I didn't understand this when I first heard it, I did the first time one of my teenagers was insisting on making a decision I knew would lead to heartache. I said to that child in all honesty, "As much as it will hurt me for you to make a decision that you know deep down is wrong, I will hurt more over the good things you will give up by making this choice. You can't have both."

We who long to give good things to our children don't even come close to the good that God would put down in the deepest recesses of our being if we would let him. We who love our children as best we can have just a taste of the love the Father lavishes on us.

That God is more concerned about our love than our failures is never seen more clearly than in the question the risen Lord asked Peter when he walked with him on the shores of Galilee after the resurrection. Peter was a broken man. In a matter of hours on the day of the crucifixion he had gone from staunchly declaring that he would stand with Jesus to the death, to cursing and denying that he ever knew the man. And now, disheartened, disillusioned, confused, he went back to what he knew best—fishing. It was here that Jesus, Peter's friend *and* his Lord, brought Peter face to face with the deepest issue of his life.

Not once did the Lord chastise Peter with the demand, "Do you promise never to deny me again?" He just asked him, "Do you love me?" (see John 21). The answer to this question would determine Peter's life from this moment on. It was not his betrayal that was the issue, but who, or what, he loved. I rather think that question echoed in Peter's heart and life as long as he lived. The question is mine and yours as well. The risen Lord, who loves us with an unfailing love, walks with us on some Galilee of our lives and asks, "Do you love me?"

Father, I hurt.
Is that a tear in your eye?

Can I really believe that you carry my burden,
*   not only in your strength,*
*   but in your heart?*

How hard it is for me to let myself believe
*   that you love me that much,*
That you would quiet me with your love,
*   and rejoice over me with singing.*

And Father,
May I not turn you away
*   in your longing to give to me*
*   gifts of true riches.*

And when you ask me if I love you,
*   I would have to answer, "Yes, Lord,*
*   but I don't love you like you love me."*
And so I would pray
*   that you would give me a love for you and your purpose*
*   that runs deeper than anything else in my life.*

Thank you for calling me
*   "my child."*

                    Amen

11
In the Hands of the Master Potter

This is the word that came to Jeremiah from the LORD: "Go down to the potter's house, and there I will give you my message." So I went down to the potter's house, and I saw him working at the wheel. But the pot he was shaping from the clay was marred in his hands; so the potter formed it into another pot, shaping it as seemed best to him. . . . "Can I not do with you as this potter does?" declares the LORD. "Like clay in the hand of the potter, so are you in my hand."

Jeremiah 18:1–4, 6

Let Him put you on His wheel and whirl you as He likes, and as sure as God is God and you are you, you will turn out exactly in accordance with the vision. Don't lose heart in the process. If you have ever had the vision of God, you may try as you like to be satisfied on a lower level, but God will never let you.

Oswald Chambers
My Utmost for His Highest

God doesn't grow great people with easy circumstances." A close friend lifted these words from one of Creath's messages and cross-stitched it for me just a few days after the accident. What she couldn't put on there was his laughter as he would add, "But most of us would settle for a little less greatness and a little more tranquility."

So true. Most of us would not mind being a saint; we just do not want to take the course for sainthood. We wouldn't mind coming out gold; we just don't want to go through the refiner's fire. And being like clay in the potter's hand doesn't appeal to us too much either. We might opt for being great if we just didn't have to *become* great.

And so we settle for the little village at the foot of the trail instead of climbing the torturous trail to the summit. Maybe we make it to the first way station, or even to the second one. But to choose, anywhere along the way, not to endure the pain of the climb is to miss the grandeur of the mountain peak.

None of us goes into the refiner's fire or onto the potter's wheel in total submission. We hold on to whatever comforts we have and cry for peace, not perfection.

As I was preparing to speak on the verse in Isaiah that declares "we are the clay, you are the potter; we are all the work of your hand" (64:8), I spent some time with a master potter learning about clay, and the difference in clay and me, and why God would choose to speak to Jeremiah at the potter's house.

Clay, this master potter said, is dug from pits and must go through a process that purifies it and gives it the elasticity and strength necessary for both the molding and the firing. The clay coming from the pits is the consistency of shale and thoroughly unusable as it is. It must be finely ground and put in a bath that allows the impurities to separate from the clay itself. After the water is drained off the clay is pressed to remove the excess water and form the clay mass. Then the clay must rest—which is understandable, I decided, after such a process! The need for rest I can relate to.

I asked the potter what happens to a piece of clay that doesn't mold in the way he had envisioned. He said if a mistake is made during the molding the clay is thoroughly kneaded and used again. "The more you work the clay," he said, "the better the piece of pottery you can make." He also said that the only real test for the clay is the firing.

As I listened, I couldn't help but think of Jeremiah when he heard, "Go down to the potter's house, and there I will give you my message" (Jer. 18:2). For the moment I was Jeremiah, wondering what the Lord might say to me through the works of this potter. It was not the pending exile of the house of Israel I took with me, as did Jeremiah, but the wonderings of my own soul. I believe the Lord gives messages not only for nations, but for his individual children as well.

And then I saw it—the difference in clay used to make pottery and the clay I am in the Potter's hands. Pottery clay is inanimate. It has no feelings, no desires, no need for comfort or attention or affirmation. It has no propensity to sin. Neither is it able to burst forth in song because the joy it feels is too good to keep inside. The clay prepared for making pottery just sits there until the potter starts the wheel turning and begins to mold the clay into the vessel he desires.

I, on the other hand, have a will of my own. I go to the wheel kicking and screaming, crying that it isn't fair and begging for at least an explanation of why I have to endure this atrocity. Unlike the silent potter's clay sitting on the resting shelf, completely pliable in the potter's hands when the wheel begins to turn, I am a real challenge. I may have to get molded, but not without a fight. I twist and turn and try so hard to wriggle free, demanding all the while, "Isn't there another way?"

And since I insist on trying to do it my way, the clay of my life has to be kneaded again and again and put back on the potter's wheel for reshaping. Could I not learn, as Jeremiah did, that the Master Potter shapes this clay that I am "as seems best to him"?

It is a message of hope to know that no matter how misshapen we become by the sufferings that tear us apart, no matter how marred by sin, no matter how hardened by repeated disappointments, the Master Potter will, each time with loving care, labor over the clay of our lives to make us into a vessel that will ultimately honor him.

None of us escapes this remaking process. Unpleasant, nay, painful as it may be, it is for our good and his glory that he takes us from the resting shelf and begins to knead himself into the clay of our lives. God's purpose in the refiner's fire or the potter's wheel is holiness. And once he begins, he does not turn back. God has his heart so set on making his children holy and righteous that no price on his part is too great and no suffering on our part will deter him. When we open ourselves to him and his purpose he will, in Christ, come into our lives and change us on the inside that we become godly men and women in this life, and in eternity we will stand in the presence of a holy and righteous God and be like him in character.

"This must be the most daring concept that has ever crossed the mind of man," Creath would say, "that the God who fashioned this vast universe would reach out to insignificant, self-centered persons as we are and offer to share his life with us. To be asked to participate in life with God himself is the greatest of all invitations." Creath would always apologize when he began to talk about what he called "God's magnificent obsession" because he said he could not tell it big enough. How can our finite minds conceive of what it really means to be called "heirs of God and co-heirs with Christ?"

Being in the hands of the Master Potter means simply that we were created in the image of God but we are being made into the likeness of Christ. That is our calling as children of God.

God would do that, I ask, with this lump of clay that I am?

It's hard to put ourselves in that picture. I may believe that you are capable of such transformation, but can I believe that about myself? Can I really believe God can mold this lump of clay into a vessel that can hold the treasures of the kingdom? Can I believe that Paul was talking about me when he said, "We have this treasure in jars of clay to show that this all-surpassing power is from God and not from us"?

It is, indeed, God who undertakes the refining and molding of our lives, who kneads into the clay that we are his love and forgiveness and grace and mercy alongside the doubts and fears and sorrows and sins that we bring to him. Unlike the inanimate clay dug from pits for making pottery, the clay that I am must face the impurities and the neediness and the sin that keeps me from being pliable in his hands.

He will not let us hide forever from the truthfulness of our inner drivenness that has one of us seeking shelter instead of openness, another of us striving to succeed at others' expense rather than seeing our lives as gifts to be spent for the building up of the kingdom, and even others of us building our lives on sand because it seems easier than constructing a life on the unrelenting rocks. When God begins a work in us, sooner or later he brings us to face not only his holiness, but our darkness.

When we choose to follow Christ, "Christ-following" Gordon MacDonald calls it, that "means in part the process of going within to the deep inner world that is dark and chaotic."[1] And this is precisely what we attempt to avoid at all costs.

Yet until we are willing to journey into these inner recesses of our hearts where we have hidden away the hurts and shames of the past they are our masters. God will always bring us to the place of opportunity to deal with what is deepest in our lives, but we can choose to invite him into the woundedness to heal us, or we can choose to quickly seal away what we cannot bear to see.

Some time ago I came to know a very gifted and talented young man who slowly began to use his giftedness for his own gain. He forgot for a while what his life was all about and wandered off into a world that vied for his allegiance. But God had begun a work in him and, through a very painful experience, reclaimed his attention.

The way back has not been easy. Restoration always requires a "resting period," which is extremely difficult for those who know they can do many things. At one point after he and I had talked at length about the sins and pains of the past, the disappointments of the present, and the uncertainty of the future, and

since I myself was at the moment walking through the valley
of some painful self-discovery, my journal became the outlet
for my thoughts, and I wrote for both of us:

Ah, Lord. Rejection hurts.
I saw it so clearly in his eyes,
This friend of mine.
He had heard "No" once again,
And I wondered . . .
How do you keep on believing in yourself
When you are constantly passed over
And the job is given to someone with lesser skills?

How do you keep on believing in your call from God
When God seems so silent?

Where do you go for courage
When you have used up your last ounce?

Where do you flee
So you can lay the burden down,
If just for a moment?

Questions, Lord.
Many more questions than answers.
But, Lord, are we even asking the right questions?

More than answers
We pray you would reveal to us the questions
That would teach us and grow us
As we wrestle with the doubt and confusion they bring.
It's a hard prayer to pray, Lord,
But don't take away the pain
Until you know we can handle the prosperity.

The valley is so deep
And the light so dim,

But when it is your light
It is enough.

Lord, we are so impatient.
We keep running ahead of you,
Calling back, "Follow me!"
We think we know what we want,
What we need.

The truth is
We know so little of ourselves.

Do we really want to know more?
Do we dare stand by
While you peel back the layers
     of acceptability
          competence
               and piety
That we have so carefully fashioned?

Yet at the same time we fear seeing
What is deepest inside,
We fear living the whole of our lives
As we are now,
     shallow
          protected
               hesitant.

Must we go to the depths
To reach the heights?
Must we be ruthlessly honest
With what drives us
Before we can be delivered from it?

Lord, this journey is much too frightening
To make alone.
You will never leave us or forsake us,
But we will be tempted to leave you.

We need another,
A friend of your own choosing
To walk the way with us.
Someone who can encourage us,
        prod us
                affirm us
As we begin to emerge
From the darkness that holds us captive.

The way to wholeness is never easy.
Take what little courage
We can gather at this moment
And begin your healing in our lives,
No matter what the cost.

Being remade isn't easy. It hurts. And it means we must go inside ourselves where it is dark and frightening. But when we walk into that darkness with our hand firmly in the hand of the One who loves us with an unfailing love and whose grace and wisdom and faithfulness can bring into that darkness the light of Christ himself, then we need not fear even the potter's wheel. For if we know the Potter, we can trust his hand. He will mold us and make us into the kind of people who can change that part of the world we touch because we will live as ones whose lives have been infused with the living Christ.

Lord,
Help us to know that the greatness you call us to
        is not that of the world;
It is not the greatness
        that is accompanied by accolades and applause.
But you call us to holiness,
And that takes a long time,
        and it is hidden to those who do not have eyes to see.

You mold the clay of our lives
And make us new creatures;
You do this by sharing your life with us.

Don't let us hide from your healing graces forever,
  even if it means walking through the darkness of our
    inner selves.
Help us to know that you are already there ahead of us,
  working for our good and your glory.

Let us one day look and see a hint of gold in our demeanor,
  a shimmer of pearl in our attitudes,
    a vessel for treasures taking shape.

And, Lord,
As we discover that we are becoming what you had intended
  all along,
  we will look back and say that the pain was worth it.
      Amen

12
Too Much for Too Long

Because so many people were coming and going that they did not even have a chance to eat, he said to them, "Come with me by yourselves to a quiet place and get some rest."

Mark 6:31

We have, indeed, to fashion our own desert where we can withdraw every day, shake off our compulsions, and dwell in the gentle healing presence of our Lord. Without such a desert we lose our own soul while preaching the gospel to others.

Henri Nouwen
The Way of the Heart

My friend, who knew me all too well, said, "There's a word for what you are describing to me." Then he went to the whiteboard in his office and on it wrote the letters B U R N O U T as he warned, "I see red lights flashing everywhere."

Not to be outdone, I replied, "Sorry, I don't have time for that. Could we call it something else?"

He said I could call it whatever I wanted but that I had been doing too much for too long and it was just a matter of time until something in me rebelled.

I walked away from him, carefully carrying with me all the reasons why I could not do things differently. And I walked right into one of the most dismal years of my life.

"Living in a crisis mode," Bill Hybels has said, "is when you spend every waking moment of every day trying to keep all the balls in the air and all the plates spinning." He talked of how we skim our energy from one compartment of our lives and flow that energy over into another in order to survive the immediate demands and by doing so deplete ourselves physically, emotionally, relationally, and spiritually. These massive energy drains, he said, leave us terribly vulnerable to sin. [1]

Interestingly, most of us when thus depleted do not first look for healthy ways to reduce the stress. We rather look for anything to make us feel better and regain a little energy so we can keep doing what we are doing. We redouble the effort. Try a little harder.

Driven by the compulsions of our society, we gather our self-esteem from our successes; we measure our success by the affirmation and approval we accumulate; and we live in denial to keep our fears of failure, of not having enough, of possible losses, from haunting our waking hours.

As I listened to Bill's message again, I realized I had been living in crisis mode for so long I thought it was the way life was supposed to be. *Doesn't everybody live this way?* I wondered.

In the years since the accident that made me a widow, I had faced so many changes in my life, my relationships, my personality, my way of doing things—all at great price—that I would wake up in the mornings wondering if I would recognize myself that day. I moved from being a rather quiet, delighted-to-be-in-the-background person to one who was suddenly having to learn to be the one called on, the one asked for opinion or counsel, the one making decisions that affected others, the one dealing with tough issues that always before I had been able to pass on to my strong husband. The challenges in my life were staggering, and I was trying desperately to prove to everyone, and especially to myself, that I could meet them all.

To complicate matters, I made a professional move that added to my life of perpetual change the responsibilities of an administrative position.

Too much for too long. Soon the rebellion began. First, my body began rebelling with total fatigue. Then my emotions began screaming for relief from the constant outflow to meet a thousand crying needs of my own to feel the pains and needs of my family, to learn how to relate on my own, to the people who crossed my path, and to fill my professional role. My spiritual life had been reduced to "God, please help." And, of course, I was doing everything I could to recoup a little of the energy so I could keep on keeping on. Somewhere in the process I lost touch with the inside of me.

About this time a friend of mine, who owns the Christian bookstore I help support by my seemingly daily purchases, put a little book by Henri Nouwen in my hands. I read *The Way of the Heart* with fatigue in my body, voices arguing in my head, and Bill Hybels' words, "The way I was doing the work of God in the world was destroying the work of God in my life," echoing in my ears.

In a section of the book called "The Furnace of Transformation" Nouwen talks about solitude as a holy place inside of us "where we gather new strength to continue the ongoing competition in life." Nouwen said:

> In solitude I get rid of my scaffolding . . . just me—naked, vulnerable, weak, sinful, deprived, broken—nothing. It is this nothingness that I have to face in my solitude, a nothingness so dreadful that everything in me wants to run to my friends, my work, and my distractions so that I can forget my nothingness and make myself believe that I am worth something. The struggle is real because the danger is real. It is the danger of living the whole of our life as one long defense against the reality of our

condition, one restless effort to convince ourselves of
our virtuousness . . . it is the struggle to die to the false
self. But this struggle is far, far beyond our own strength.
Anyone who wants to fight his demons with his own
weapons is a fool. The wisdom of the desert is that the
confrontation with our own frightening nothingness
forces us to surrender ourselves totally and uncondi-
tionally to the Lord Jesus Christ.[2]

Reading those words very late one night, I found myself
off my bed and on my knees (which made quite an impres-
sion on me, and probably God, too, because I didn't do that
very often) and said, "O God, I'm doing this all wrong, aren't
I? Isn't all my busyness and my performance my way of con-
vincing myself I am okay? My way of proving I can make it?
And, Lord, I'm so weary."

Back on the bed I wrote the prayer I was feeling in my
deepest being:

> Lord, I'm trying to fix myself, aren't I? I'm running to
> doctors to tell me what to do so I can feel better. Even with
> some counseling, Lord, I am digging up the "acceptable"
> ills inside—those that make me look sinned against. All
> this in an effort to look good and feel good. Because if I
> can get back to my normal busy life I can continue to flee
> the ugly truth—that down inside of me, at the core of my
> being, there is an unending battle for who is going to sit
> on the throne—me or you?
>
> Oh, Lord. How can I be so blind? Everything in me is
> screaming, "Slow down! Bow down! Give it up!" But my
> pride keeps me washing my face instead of letting you
> wash my soul.
>
> God, please don't let me live my whole life in defense
> against the reality of my inner sinfulness.

I really want to know you. But I can never know you in all truth as long as I cling so tenaciously to my perceived securities. Yet in any moment of truth I know the pursuit of these so-called securities to be a chasing after the wind. They are only shadows that disappear with reality. They are vapor that is dissipated in adversity, illusions that cannot bear close scrutiny.

Dear God, do I dare pray that you would peel back the layers of piety that I have so carefully fashioned? Can I withstand even a glimpse of the self-centered compulsions of my inner life?

Tomorrow I may—No. Tomorrow I *will* cry out in protest that it is too painful and I can't go through it. But to-night please hear me as I ask you to hold my hand tightly and start me on the journey to wholeness. And when I keep trying to turn back, please stand in the way and keep urging me on. Give me the grace to believe in you and the desire to follow you wherever the road may lead. Because Lord, I do want to know you in the center of my life. I want to love you from the very depths of my heart. And I want to serve you because I can do no other.

Lord, hear me now. Not because I'm strong enough to face it, but because I'm desperate enough to want it. Please walk me through the anger and resentment and selfishness and all the unnamed demons that I have so pridefully dressed up to look presentable.

And Lord. Just when I think I can't stand anymore, give me the courage to again pray for wholeness, no matter what it costs.

Burnout is perhaps an overused word, but still aptly de-scribes the feeling of having given until the well is completely dry and then continuing to do what is demanded even when there is nothing left to give. Here we become vulnerable to the seduction of whatever feels good. To succumb to anything that offers a quick escape poses a threat to our health, our jobs, our relationships, and our spiritual journey.

How do we find the energy to fight the fatigue, the depression, the despair that most often accompany such a dark place? Is there any real hope when the devastation of the storm is so extensive?

Yes. As long as there is life, there is hope. Just one little spark inside that keeps whispering, "Hang in there, don't give up," if we will listen to it, is enough to keep us from giving in to the deceiver who would have us believe it is all over. There is hope—and there is help.

As Nouwen says, we would be fools to try to fight our demons with only our own weapons. There was a significant spiritual dimension to the battle I was fighting, but to "just pray about it," as I was often advised to do, was only the first step toward healing for me. The physical, emotional, and relational dimensions of my life had been sorely neglected and needed to be tended with the same diligence I would give to my spiritual life. I did not get into this condition in a day, and I had come to realize that I would likely not get out of it quickly or easily. Indeed, it took many months and involved making some very tough choices. It took clinging tenaciously to what I believed about God even when I could not feel his presence. And it took coming to accept that my needing help to weather this storm did not reflect a lack of faith.

The help I needed was provided by four professionals. I was fortunate enough to have an internist who cared enough about me to argue with me about the use of a mild antidepressant after he found nothing in any of my medical tests to warrant looking further for a physical reason for my extreme fatigue. He finally said to me, "I think you think it is not okay to be depressed."

But before I would consider the medication I met with a psychiatrist to ask him to please explain to me why an antidepressant working on something in my brain could make my aching body feel better. He patiently drew diagrams for me, explaining that the medication would balance the neurotransmitters in my brain that affect the functioning of every area of our physical and emotional being. With the correction of the chemical imbalance that very often accompanies long-term stress, the physical body then begins to readjust itself, and the depleted emotional energies can begin rebuilding. A Christian himself, he helped me take my depression out of the spiritual realm in this particular instance.

A wise and wonderful chiropractor, another longtime Christian, helped me recover from a very old injury that had been aggravated by the accumulated stress, and in the process he became my greatest encourager. And a Christian therapist helped me put all of this together as he gently and patiently walked me through all the rooms inside of me that I had over the years stuffed full of hurts and fears and guilt and overused negative tapes.

I found that God reached out to me through all these professionals—and through a persistent little voice deep inside me that kept reminding me there really is a lot of life left to live.

When we wake up one day and realize we are dying a slow death, we must ruthlessly confront the stresses and emotional drains, that push us to the edge of burnout. We musk ask the living Lord, who calls us to abide in him, to teach us the rhythm of our own lives and give us the grace to balance our work, rest, worship, and play so that we can radiate his love and peace to the hurrying and exhausted world around us.

Lord,
we forget that the human body
can run on empty emotions only so long.

*Help us to heed the warnings you give us along the way
that would save us from reaching such depletion
of body, soul, and spirit.*

*Help us to build into our lives those quiet moments with you
that would keep us attuned to your loving guidance.*

*And help us build into our lives those relationships
that would hold us accountable to wise choices.*
                              Amen

13
Quiet Desperation

May our Lord Jesus Christ himself and God our Father, who loved us and by his grace gave us eternal encouragement and good hope, encourage your hearts and strengthen you in every good deed and word.

2 Thessalonians
2:16

The mind can descend far lower than the body . . . flesh can bear only a certain number of wounds and no more, but the soul can bleed in ten thousand ways and die over and over again each hour.

Charles Spurgeon,
quoted in *More Than
Coping* by Elizabeth
Skoglund

Depression is an insidious usurper of life. And it is no respecter of persons. It grips the rich and the poor, the young and the old, the learned and the unlearned, the strong and the weak, the Christian and the atheist. With its long tentacles of self-doubt it slowly squeezes down on the spirit until its prey is convinced there is no way to ever be free. Death begins to look like a welcome relief, if only it would come. But this death is slow, progressive, inch by inch, and therein may lie its downfall—the victim may get tired of the dying and ask for help.

Depression has almost caught up with the common cold as being the most common ailment in twentieth-century America. It is the illness of the nineties. It has become big business for the counseling field, both secular and Christian, and has spawned an abundance of books. It is hailed as the catchall diagnosis for the tired and weary by some skeptics and denounced by some religionists as a tool of Satan to keep the devout from dealing with their spiritual waywardness. It is often scoffed at by those who have never experienced a debilitating melancholy, and it is feared by the loved ones of those who suffer recurring anxiety attacks. For those who have struggled with depression, it is suffering as real as that of a wound in the body.

The sources of depression are legion, and its cures are illusive. Its definitions fill medical journals. It can be as mild as a temporary "blue mood" created by any life change, and it can be severe enough to lead to hospitalization or self-destruction. It can be caused by the loss of a loved one, the loss of economic security, or the loss of status. It can accompany long-term stress that builds due to coping with work, life, and relationships. It can be caused by personal choices gone wrong or by moral compromise. And in some people it can be brought on by nothing definable at all.

Body and spirit are so integrated that what affects one affects the other. What begins as a disease in the spirit, if left unattended, will eventually be felt in the body. Certain physical disorders and chemical imbalances within the body's systems may cause moodiness, despondency, or even anxiety long before physical symptoms appear. A prolonged illness or the body's having to adjust to physical changes or to fight chronic pain usually results in some degree of depression. Fear, anger, and depression forced into hiding over a long period of time will often impair the body's physical functioning in some way. Since body and spirit affect each other so greatly, any attempt to deal with the emotional issues of depression must also consider the possible need for medical attention.

Quite possibly what makes depression such a menacing adversary is the sense of failure it brings. The blackest black in the universe is the emptiness that descends when we have written "hopeless" across the landscape of our lives. When we invest our problems with power to dictate our future, we have given them the place of God, and we quickly begin to lose our way. But the word *hopeless* is never applied to us by our Creator; he tells us there is always hope. When our body and spirit are subjected to massive drains of energy and emotion, we become depleted physically and emotionally. However deep the fatigue, however dark the thoughts, there is hope and there is help. Always.

I know both the dark and the hope. I know what it is like to come to the point where life is so much effort you don't care if you live another day. And I know what it is like to cling to a tiny thread of hope.

When I first heard someone talk of "quiet desperation" many years ago, I shrugged my shoulders and thought, *Isn't that normal?* I gave the term my own definition: "quiet because no one knows; desperation because one slip will plunge me into an abyss I will never survive." I lived with a floating anxiety that required enormous inner control just to keep myself from spending every waking moment cowering in any corner that offered me a little security. I became a master at disguising fear as acceptable protection, inadequacy as competence, perfectionism as a job well done, and compliance to everyone else's wishes as commitment to my roles in life.

It was this ability to fake it on the surface for so long that kept me from facing the enemy within that was destroying me piece by piece. My enemy was not the depression that finally rendered me unable to cope with my life and my world any longer without some help; my real enemy was that the weaknesses masqueraded as strengths so successfully.

The floating anxiety eventually attached itself to my fear of doing or even saying something that might cause harm to someone else, and I became uncontrollably afraid of handling food. My hands could never be clean enough, the refrigerator could never be cold enough, the food could never be fresh enough, my preparation could never be adequate for absolute safe eating. I washed my hands countless times a day and still threw out perfectly good food because I couldn't be sure if I had remembered to wash my hands before preparing or handling it. This is not fun to admit; it was even less fun to have lived this way. But this phobia was the catalyst that pushed me into admitting that my controls were breaking down and there were some things inside of me that needed attention.

At its worst, though I was still outwardly coping with all of the responsibilities I had both at home and in my career and covering my fears masterfully, inwardly I was slowly giving up. I had lost a great deal of weight I didn't have to lose, and I was disappearing to the bedroom as soon as I could. There I would sit in the dark, begging God to cure me or let me be locked up so I couldn't hurt my family with my food.

This was the time in my walk of faith that I dealt with anger toward God. I couldn't understand why, when I was doing everything I knew to do spiritually, physically, and emotionally, he couldn't—or wouldn't—make me better. I struggled with whether I even believed he was there; and if he was there, if he even cared. I prayed, I begged, I cried—I quit.

One night while sitting in the dark knowing I couldn't go on like this, I got up and turned on the light and began to write my "resignation" prayer to him—-the prayer that gave it all to him whether or not I ever got well. I just couldn't carry it anymore.

Then I quit praying about the problem because it seemed that my praying had simply become an extension of my worrying. So I grasped at something I had heard Creath say in a retreat once, and I clung to it like a lifeline. When I would feel myself beginning to choke with fright I would say, "God, please help me to believe what Creath said, that 'You can trust in the character of God beyond what you can understand.' Because if that's not true, I have no hope." That and no more was my prayer, over and over and over.

This all surfaced before counseling was easily available outside a medical setting, and it was especially frowned on by the religious community. But through some personal contacts in the professional field I was able to talk through some of these terrors over a few weeks and at least begin to peek more honestly and openly at the factors that were creating such anxiety in my life. However, continued therapy was not possible, and I ended up having to figure out, alone, what to do with whatever I was finding. The only thing that made me willing to keep trying was what I wrote on that piece of paper after I wrote my resignation prayer that night. I called them my three reasons to live: (1) Surely God had something better than this planned for my life, (2) I loved Creath too much to die, and (3) My children deserved better from me than what they were getting. It was a beginning, a good beginning, and there were some significant changes over the next few years.

But depression visited me again. What had begun needed to be finished. While I had regained my will to live and had begun to look at the things inside me, I had touched only the tip of the iceberg. Underneath were the driving forces that I had dressed up to look more acceptable than the handwashing and the sitting in the dark, but they were driving me, nonetheless.

By this time I was older, with much more life experience. I had learned that God could be trusted beyond what I could understand, my children were grown, and I had grieved long and hard the death of the most important person in my life. Just as I thought I was going on pretty well with my life, I was blindsided by a combination of burnout, extreme physical fatigue from several years of accumulated stress, and a relational experience that let me know everything about me was changing and the old way of living and relating wasn't working anymore.

This time, with the help of a wise and gifted counselor, I began chipping away at the iceberg. Of course, what I asked of him in the beginning was how to regain my energy and get back to my old self, which, for all its downfalls, was at least familiar. I didn't want this setback to last very long, and I didn't want anyone to know that I didn't have my life all together and needed someone to help me gather myself up. I just wanted the counselor to work on the depression and make me feel better.

What he knew, and what I later learned, was that the depression was only a symptom, the outer result of an inner rebellion. It was as if both my body and my spirit had conspired to let me know that if I intended to live the rest of my life according to the dictates of my inner compulsions, it was going to be a short and desperate life.

With the counselor's encouragement I began to name the things I had spent years stuffing down into the well-polished brass pot I envisioned inside of me, the one I had expended so much energy keeping the lid on so no one, especially me, would know what was inside.

At times I felt relief that at last I could identify the enemy so I had something to fight. At other times I only felt defeat. One day I would see clearly the anger and personal desires I had buried in order to keep peace at any price, and I would recognize the payment exacted for this much pseudo-peace. The next day I would deny it all.

Anytime I began to feel a little strength and confidence, I would have to do battle with words like *pride* and *selfish*. Then, just when I would think I could sink no further, another fear or guilt or failure—real or perceived—would raise its ugly head, and I would have to decide again if I was going to face this one too.

So many times I wanted to give up. The work of therapy was too hard and too painful. "What if I go through all this and nothing changes?" I cried to the counselor. "What if I go back to all my old ways of thinking and feeling and dealing with life? Why go through this if it is not going to make any real difference?"

Patiently he said to me, "You've come too far. You couldn't go back now even if you wanted to. As you come to a strong sense of your own worth, the changes will come."

Silently and tearfully I wrestled with the good news/bad news of what he had just said. The good news was that I had broken through enough of the old compulsions that they could no longer hold the same power over me. The bad news was that I had to trudge on through whatever else was still there, however painful it might be.

Then he asked "Will you let me help you?"

I had been somewhat resistant to this whole counseling experience to this point, but with his question it was as if a dam broke inside me, and the intensity of the emotions told me I already had crossed an invisible line. Without being aware of when it happened, I had chosen *life,* and no matter how hard, how long, or how painful the process, I wanted to be free of the bondage I had lived under all these years.

It was a long way down, and it was a long way back up. But I'm glad I made the trip. This was a lonely journey, because even with the guidance and encouragement of a skilled and caring counselor and with a trusted friend I could talk to about anything, no one could go inside with me. When we walk among the demons that spring up amid the terrors we banned from our consciousness long ago, we have to do so without the companionship of any other human being. We are fortunate if we have family and friends who can hear us and love us and have patience with us through this time, but the battle itself is fought in a place where only God can accompany us. And when we somehow find the courage to choose health and wholeness and we ask God to hold us tightly and walk with us into the darkness, he will make the impossible possible.

As we tend to do with anything that hurts, the first thing we do in the face of depression is try to find ways to escape it—and if we can't escape it, at least to fix it. But, as with all suffering, we must lean into the pain and pay the price for healing.

We may get by for a while by hiding the depression and finding immediate, though temporary, relief. We may get by with this dance for years, but each time we force the issues inward to hide the depression from ourselves and everyone else, the fuse leading to the dynamite burns a little shorter. Eventually, depression demands attention.

If we can rid the word *depression* of its negative reputation and the shame that is often attached to it, we will then treat it as we do any other pain that invades our life, and we will seek renewed health. Our minds, like our bodies, attempt to take care of themselves by telling us something needs proper attention, and it is right for us to respond to that cry for help. It is not unspiritual to seek help for our emotional well-being.

Depression, however mild or severe, needs to be taken seriously and tended caringly. I still recognize the feeling of "quiet desperation" from time to time in my life, but no longer do I greet it with a shrug of the shoulders. I may again in my life face a depression that will require intervention, I don't know. But I do know that I will take a very different me into whatever new challenge my life brings. I know, too, that even depression is a tool that God would use for our good. He would work in and through the depression to free us from the buried terrors that would strangle us, and he would set our feet on high places so we might again serve him.

The way through any depression, whether it is serious enough to require professional intervention or mild enough to respond to with our own wise and careful attention, is to open it to the healing work of God. David Allen, in his book *In Search of the Heart,* says that "the first and basic step to discovery is love. We must be open to the sustaining power of God's love, the creative, redemptive, healing force of life."[1]

"As you come to a strong sense of your own worth . . ." Those words were said to me over and over again. As we take hold of the truth that our lives have been infused with worth and value by God himself, and we are loved by God with an unfailing, everlasting love, then we can begin to believe down in our souls that we have the very resources we need for health and wholeness and strength of character. With God it is not a matter of bringing in something from the outside to bear on the problem; it is the releasing of what is already within us. We may need some help to unshackle these traits of the One in whose image we are made, but in coming to the place where we boldly believe we are loved and valued even when the depression will not let us feel so, we become what Allen calls "missionaries to our own hearts."

Depression exposed to the light of God's love and met with the courage inherent in a strong sense of our own worth will not ultimately defeat us. We will be, as the apostle Paul said, "transformed by the *renewing* of our minds" (Romans 12:12).

Dear Lord,
Sometimes we feel defeated by life.

The sun doesn't shine for us anymore
and a sense of foreboding awakens us every morning.
Nothing feels good, we can't think clearly or normally,
and we are sure it will never be better.

We don't know how to pray.

Take the word "hopeless" from us.
Lord, just a little hope can go a long way.

Give us the courage to believe that being made in your image
means that we have worth
and value
and dignity,

*And give us the courage to walk into the inner recesses of our
     lives
     and expose all of the fear and guilt and compulsions
          hidden there
          to the light of your love and forgiveness and grace.*

*In our depression, Lord,
Lead us to those who can help us
     as you heal us.*

                              Amen

14
Letting Go

Forget the former things;
do not dwell on the past.
See, I am doing a new thing!
Now it springs up; do you not perceive it?
I am making a way in the desert
and streams in the wasteland.

Isaiah 43:18–19

Life and faith always insist on moving forward; and I cannot
move forward without leaving something behind. . . . To let go
of what one is holding on to is no small matter. . . . The trapeze
artist . . . must let go of one trapeze just at the right moment,
to hover for a moment in the void before catching hold of the
other trapeze.

Paul Tournier
A Place for You

The living of life has inherent in it a series of "little deaths," the giving up of one way of being or thinking or relating in order to attain a higher level. Sometimes we must give up unhealthy ways; sometimes simply outgrown ways. This is never more true than in the losses in our lives when the unexpected, unwanted, and painful changes are forced upon us and we, in our fear of the unknown, cling to the familiar, or to the memory of what we had. In major losses our identity, our security, our perceptions, our dreams, our relationships, indeed, the whole of our lives change, and we must let go of what we cannot keep. We must turn loose of the past and the things that tend to hold us captive even after they are long gone.

Soon after the accident, someone gave me a piece of paper on which she had copied something she had seen on a wall hanging: "In times of trouble, some people grow wings, others buy crutches." At the time I was hobbling around on crutches and not at all sure wings were even a possibility. I think when life has fallen apart and we are not sure how to go on with what fragments are left, emotional crutches which help give some sense of stability as we wander through the debris left by a lifestorm are a necessary and welcome commodity. For a while we desperately need something to support the extra burdens we are suddenly carrying, burdens added by the shock of loss, decisions that have to be made wisely and speedily, by heaviness of heart, by grieving friends and loved ones who need our comfort, and even by the feeling of not wanting to go on.

Some crutches are fashioned from healthy material, others from material that assures only more heartache and is extremely difficult to release. But the danger of even a *good* thing is that it can become the enemy of the *best* thing. To depend too long on whatever crutches serve us well is to stunt the growth of the wings we are all capable of having. Then the very things that helped us get through the tough times, although good in themselves, become our prison.

While letting go of these crutches is sometimes simply attempting a few steps now and then, agonizing though they may be, until we get to the place in our journey where the crutches are no longer needed, sometimes letting go requires burning the crutches. I have had experience with both situations.

Letting go of Creath was very hard, and it took a very long time. I needed him for my life to make sense—at least I needed the memory of him. I needed his identity, if not as his wife, then as his widow, while I was learning how to walk with half of me gone. I needed to be Mrs. Creath Davis until I could sign my name *Verdell Davis* without having to think about it. I needed to talk about him until the richness we had together mellowed into my inner being and no longer needed expression to be real. I needed to share his books and quote from his teaching until I could accept that the wonderful things we all who were touched by his ministry had learned from him belonged now to all and they were ours to give. I needed to hold on to him while I wrestled with the issues of faith and trust and who God is in the darkness.

Somewhere along the way, letting him go became a choice I had to make.

I let go of Creath one small step at a time. Each step at the moment seemed inconsequential and left me with no feeling of having gained anything. But as these tiny steps carried me forward and as I kept reaching out to touch whatever piece of new life I could feel, I found one day I could say that Creath had taken his rightful place in my life. The life we shared is a part of who I am and whoever I will become, but he is not my present and he is not my future.

He is an easy part of family conversations now, and there is not a day that I don't think about him. The grandchildren, one of whom was born after he died, talk often about the things they have learned about their grandfather. I sometimes find them looking at his pictures and telling each other that he died in an airplane crash and he is in heaven. They ask me to tell them stories about him over and over again. Brittany, the firstborn, cooed and giggled and toddled her way into her grandfather's heart. He was with her almost every day after she was nine months old until his death. Brittany was only eighteen months old when he died, but she has surprised us with an unusual affection and warmth for her grandfather and with memories that go beyond the things we have told her. He is a real person to his grandchildren and not just an untouchable picture on the wall.

The memories for all of us are precious, and memories are just what they are. We have let him go—and he is ours forever.

Letting go of the ministry we were in for more than twenty years was another step I had to take, and I thought I was ready for it. My oldest son, David, the Christian Concern board, and I worked diligently to continue the activities we had become accustomed to as believers, but in time our own personal responsibilities made it necessary for us to seek someone to fill the position as director of the ministry. When the time actually came that I sat in Kaleo Lodge and, for the first time in the four years since his death, listened to someone other than Creath introduce the retreat as the new director of Christian Concern Foundation, I could hardly hold in the sobs that were threatening to drown me. I was not prepared for it to hurt as much as it did. For several months following I grieved the giving up of a place and a ministry that had been the fulfillment of Creath's call to be God's servant, and therefore a place and a ministry that had been a great part of the fulfillment of my life as his wife.

Creath saw his calling from the Lord as that of a discipler. He saw himself as the coach, and the lay men and women as the players called by God to carry the good news of love and hope wherever they went. His place was to walk through the everydayness of their lives with them, to love and encourage and counsel them, to laugh with them and cry with them, to rejoice with them on the mountaintops and mourn with them in the valleys, to help them do this with each other and experience what it is like to be in community. And this he did well. But most of all, for those of us who sat at his feet, he gave us a vision of the majesty and glory of Jesus Christ and the awesome wonder of being a child of God. This did not die with him.

I grieve still the scattering of a fellowship of believers molded into a family by years of sharing a common life journey. This was extended family, a loosely knit fellowship of people diverse in age, denominational affiliation, professional achievement, economic comforts, and other loyalties, all held together by two things—our hunger to know and follow Jesus Christ, and our commitment to each other.

We were people who together had forged our faith, raised our children, buried our loved ones, walked through heartaches none of us could have carried alone, celebrated our triumphs made so much sweeter in the sharing, mourned our losses, and laughed until we cried and cried until we could laugh again. It was in this strong sense of community, *koinonia* is the word, I think, that we learned how to love, how to be vulnerable, how to encourage each other, how to embrace our hurting neighbors, and how to be God's people as we lived our daily lives.

These friendships have never wavered, but the gathering together we did for so many years before, and then through a time of corporate grief, was one of those pieces of life that had to be released. As I drove home from one of our last times of meeting as a Christian Concern fellowship, crying as I thanked God for the richness of the things we had learned in the past and were learning now of his love and faithfulness, I had to pull over into the parking lot of an office complex and write on a wedding invitation lying in the seat beside me the words that kept coming with the tears.

> Lord,
> We have come to you so many times in these last days,
> Days that have stretched into months and years.
> We have brought to you such heavy hearts and blinding needs
> And we have struggled with your sovereignty and your
>   perfect will
>   in our world of senseless tragedies, personal trauma,
>   and shattered dreams.

But Lord, when we have been tempted to seek easy answers
    to our questions
        and quick cures for our hurts
We have oft echoed the words of Peter
        as you asked the disciples if they, too, would turn away
        when the answers weren't easy and the cures were
            painful.
Because, Lord, "Where would we go? You alone have the
    words of life."

In our brokenness we have heard your words with new ears
        and seen your ways with new eyes.
We have been opened to new depths of commitment
        and moved to new heights of praise.

Lord, as you heal us, you again put our feet on high places
        and cause us to look beyond our now to your eternity.
We feel the breath of fresh life
        and know most assuredly that you still have plans
            for us.

And, Father, as our faltering steps become more steady
Never let us forget the things we learned in the valley.
It was in the valley that we learned to walk by faith and not
    by sight.
        It was in the valley that we learned joy in the absence
            of happiness.
        It was in the valley that we learned the richness of our
            relationships.

So now, Lord, we come to you with humbled hearts.
We see clearly that even when we questioned your ways
        and doubted your love
You patiently gave us your grace and your peace.
        You have shown us your goodness in unmistakable ways.

> You have been the spring of living water in the desert
>   of our despair;
> You have called forth the music hidden in the depths
>   of our souls.
>
> Father, we bow before you in awe and wonder.
> We praise you for allowing us to taste of your greatness.
> We long for the day we will see you, Lord, in all your
>   majesty and glory.
> But, until that day,
>   we will journey on
>   in the light of your redeeming love.

Days did indeed stretch into months and years, and I became weary of changes and challenges and testing and growing pains. It seemed that every time I came through a stretch of new territory and thought surely I could rest awhile, I would look up and see a sign that read: "No Parking."

A third major letting-go experience came for me at such a time. I was learning to think of my life without Creath and the ministry as my life-definers, but I could not yet think of my life without a professional identity. It took a civil war inside myself to convince me I couldn't live the rest of my life clinging to what was familiar and secure. The battle was intense.

I spent many years in a profession I loved, twenty-two of them in the private school system of one of the largest churches in Dallas. The director of that school for the first twenty years I was there, as well as the faculty and staff, became family to me, and working there felt like home.

I wore many hats at the school and eventually did what I loved most: help develop programs to meet the special learning needs of the younger child and train teachers to work with these children and their parents. I was always challenged and fulfilled by the constant growth within the school, both in enrollment and in the programs we offered, and the opportunities I had for involvement with other professionals and organizations in the city. So when the accident happened and everything in my life began to change, this was the one thing that seemed to never change, and it afforded me a great deal of comfort.

But as it is with everything in life, things did not remain the same forever. When the director retired, I became director of the school and with that position moved on to the Christian education staff of the church. Soon after, a restlessness and an exhaustion set in that I found very hard to explain and harder to deal with. I knew I had reason to be tired because not only was I feeling the stress of years of grief and having to learn to live again, but the job itself demanded a great deal of time and energy. The tension finally turned to total fatigue, and I could no longer pretend it was just going to go away. I began to consider leaving the last place that defined my life as I had known it for so many years. But what would such a change do to my fragile new self? The battle raged on.

When I finally began to analyze what was going on inside of me and not just blame the circumstances around me for the depression I was battling, I knew something much deeper than the issue of grief and the expectations of the job was at stake. I finally came to accept the disturbing fact that I was being led out of my professional position to follow what appeared to be little more than a dream. I was doing the job well, and while there was no logical reason for me to quit, inside of me a voice was crying out for me to unlock my heart and at least listen to its pleas.

So finally I sat down with some trusted friends and asked them to help me make some sense out of the conflicting messages between my head and my heart.

One very strong voice inside my head seemed to be saying loudly, "How can you possibly consider leaving a job where you get much-needed affirmation, not to mention the security it offers? It gives you a place to belong and at least guarantees that you will have a group of people to relate to on a regular basis. Will there be anybody in your life when you are out there on your own? And since your worth and value come from how well you perform, if you leave this job, how will you prove you are okay so you can feel good about yourself? You have proven that you can succeed at your profession—you haven't proven you can succeed at life! And you will really be out there *alone.*"

Another, much quieter but very insistent voice came from my heart. It pleaded, "Your life has changed. Your world is changing. It's okay to go with it. What about that dream? What about asking God to let you write someday? Could that someday be now?"

The job was secure, safe, and familiar. And logic told me to stay. The world I felt calling me was undefined, risky—and scary. The two voices were relentless. But I often had whispered to my grandchildren, "It'll be an *adventure,*" when they were feeling a little uncertain about trying something new.

So, contrary to the me I had known all these years, the me who craved a security blanket, I chose adventure. And like the trapeze artist who must let go of one swing and hover for a moment in the void before catching the other bar, I let go of the trapeze I was holding without another one clearly in sight.

Elisabeth Elliot made the world aware of the profound wisdom her young missionary husband had shown when he said, not long before he was killed by the Auca Indians, "He is no fool who gives what he cannot keep to gain what he cannot lose." The life we so carefully guard and protect does not belong to us, but the choice we make for our souls is eternal. The things of this life, whether they give us pain or pleasure, are transitory, and we only have what is left inside us after the things themselves are gone.

Letting go is never easy, but we are all called to hold, with open hands, life and the things in it, even if they are the crutches that have held us up,
    the familiar that has given us comfort,
        the loved one who has given us joy,
            the child who has given us pleasure
                or the child who has given us pain;
whether it be a situation we cannot change,
    an identity that is no longer ours,
        a relationship that won't heal,
            a home we must leave,
                or unhealthy beliefs that hold us captive.

We become the prisoner of what we cannot let go. We become the possessor of what we give away.

Lord, it's so hard to let go of the things we want,
    or think we want;
The things we need,
    or think we need;
The things that make us feel secure
    or loved,
        or wanted;
The things that give us affirmation.

We reach out for those things
    that have been wrenched away from us,
        and bring back only air.

We clutch to our hearts the things that feel familiar,
    and miss the adventure that awaits us
        when our hands are free.

Lord, don't let us so shut ourselves in
to what we know,
or what we had,
or what we wish for,
That we lose our dreams.

Give us courage.

Letting go is so hard.
                                        Amen

15
Life Is Gift

*The LORD God formed the man from the dust of the ground
and breathed into his nostrils the breath of life, and the man
became a living being. . . .
In his hand is the life of every creature
        and the breath of all mankind. . . .
Man's days are determined;
        you have decreed the number of his months
and have set limits he cannot exceed. . . .
If it were his intention
        and he withdrew his spirit and breath,
all mankind would perish together
        and man would return to the dust.*

Genesis 2:7; Job
12:10; 14:5; 34:14

*Life is gift—pure, simple, sheer gift—and we here on earth
are to relate to it accordingly.*

John Claypool
*Tracks of a Fellow
Struggler*

S ometimes priceless treasures come our way in plain
wrapping. Such a package arrived in my life in 1974 in
the form of a small book sent to us by the publisher just
as it was released.

Word Books, as the publishing company was known at the
time, was always sending us new releases, and for a book lover

like me that meant hours of letting the dishes go, leaving the
beds unmade, encouraging the kids to find something fun to
do, and forgetting to start supper until it was time to eat. This
particular delivery contained a book written by John Claypool,
a fellow minister Creath had met. Although I had not met him,
I knew something of his story and was eager to read his book,
but we were leaving for a few days at the ranch to build fence
and "tend cattle," and reading was not on Creath's agenda.

I decided to take the book with me anyway, just in case he
let me have a little time off. Well, I made the mistake of starting the book in the car on the way to West Texas. I ended up
sitting in the middle of the corral reading when I was supposed
to be keeping the branding iron ready for the next calf. The
book had captured me, and I was its willing slave.

What I had no way of knowing then was that that book
was to become my teacher and my discipler without my being
aware of its impact on me; it would become my friend and
encourager in the darkest hours of my life.

The book, *Tracks of a Fellow Struggler,* touched me at a level
that was much deeper than an empathy for the sorrow of
Claypool's loss. The story itself was compelling and brought tears
that became sobs as I read of the discovery of Laura Lou's leukemia, the remission, the relapse, her suffering as the dying child,
and his suffering as the helpless father. But it was what Claypool
was saying about God that took up residence inside of me and
forced to the surface some questions and fears I had kept safely
locked away because they were too painful to think about.

I married Creath when I was eighteen, just after my first
semester in college, and we spent the first eight years of our
marriage finishing college while pastoring a church, starting
seminary, having our first two children, teaching school, and,
in our mid-twenties, moving to Dallas to start a new ministry.
There was never another love in my life than Creath, and for
the almost twenty-eight years we were married I just would not
contemplate the possibility of life without him.

But in life the unthinkable happens. Unspeakable tragedy turns our world upside down. Unbearable pain threatens to rob us of all desire to live. Feelings of hopelessness, anger, loneliness, confusion, and doubt cause us to question even those things we have held sacred. Any thoughts of the future are filled with apprehension. Seemingly impossible choices loom up menacingly, and we just do not have the energy to keep on keeping on.

As I sorted through the debris of that terrible lifestorm, I instinctively picked up *Tracks of a Fellow Struggler* to again read what John Claypool had taught me. In this reading of it I knew I had internalized so many of those things I had reflected on over the thirteen years the book had been part of me. And when I had stood on that grave some months earlier and realized I had been given an incredible gift to have been the one to walk through Creath's life and ministry with him for well over half my life, I was no longer just quoting John Claypool, saying, "Life is gift"; that bit of truth had become mine. And it was to show itself in some surprising ways.

I learned through my own experience, and through the experience of others who trusted me with their painful stories, that we almost always succumb to focusing all of our attention on what we have lost, even though the pieces of what we have left are begging to be revived. We deprive ourselves of the beauty of the rainbow because we are looking only at the flood waters left by the storm.

It is a double tragedy to reduce the significance of those people closest to us by focusing only on the one we have lost. In the loss of a child, for instance, the temptation is to try to make another child in the family "take the place" of the one who died, or to almost ignore the remaining child by continually talking about all the assets of the other. Or in the loss of a spouse, to talk as if life is now over and there is nothing left to live for. And when a prominent position has been terminated, and with it the prestige and security we had come to depend upon, it is easy to withdraw into bitterness and let die the gifts and abilities that got us into that position in the first place.

All too often we do as I have seen over and over in my work with special-needs young children; when frustrated because what they are doing does not look like they want it to, they tend to destroy the whole project. Likewise we, grown-ups that we are, can become so disheartened over the fragments of a shattered dream lying around us that we build a bonfire and throw into it both the dream and the things we can learn from those pieces that are left.

So I came to see that my life with Creath was gift, pure and simple. I did not deserve it and did nothing to earn it. But the pain of losing that gift clouded what was close at hand. I loved my children and knew they loved me, but it was difficult to be with them without feeling so painfully the absence of their father. And the grandchildren, brand-new at life, brought enormous anguish each time they would take a first step, say a new word, and do all the things growing infants and toddlers delight our hearts with, because I knew they would never know their grandfather.

I found myself pulling back a little from the closeness of the family to try to protect my own bleeding wound just a little. But even so, the going on with life put us together quite often. And there were those long, late-night telephone conversations. I tried to be honest and open about what was going on in me, and I encouraged my sons and daughter to talk, if not with me at least with someone, about their pain and anger and questions and confusion. And about life, their life, with all its hopes and dreams altered by this unexpected and unplanned-for intrusion.

We talked, and as time went on I was able to begin to see them without my protective covering, and I well remember at one point the thought flooded over me that, yes, I had lost their father, but I had them in a deeper way than ever before. A new and different bonding took place between us as they showed their concern for me and each in his or her own way tried to ease my pain.

My heart was warmed at the good things I saw going on in each of them as they struggled with overwhelming grief and with taking on some responsibilities much sooner than they had anticipated they would. After one time together when this was so evident, I came home and broke the silence in the emptiness of my house with the exclamation, "My treasures! They truly are my treasures!" No longer could I only see what I had lost; I could clearly see what I still had.

"Life is gift, and we must respond to it accordingly," wrote Claypool. On the heels of seeing my children as earthly treasures that were mine to cherish, I knew assuredly that they were indeed gift, that I must not hold them too tightly or I would squeeze the life out of them and at the same time deny myself the pleasure of their being because I would be so afraid of losing them.

I called it the "loss of innocence" the day I put Shawna in her car to drive back to college over roads still a little icy from the latest winter freeze. Then, sometime during her three-hour drive (while I was trying to keep my mind occupied with other thoughts), a stab of reality drove its way through my head and my heart: *Accidents no longer happen to other people.* It had happened to me once, and it could happen again. I had absolutely no guarantee that I would never have another loss in my life. God in his graciousness had given me Creath; in his wisdom he had taken him, and in his grace he was bringing healing into my pain.

Indeed, as Jeremiah said, "I know, O LORD, that a man's life is not his own; it is not for man to direct his steps" (Jer. 10:23). Interestingly, I did not feel panic, I felt gratitude that I was learning what God can do with us when we even haltingly trust him to get us through the storm.

The truth that life is gift had once again made itself known to me. And from that time on I have been able to pray for my children's health and safety, for their spouses and my grandchildren, and then go about my business and not sit with my hand on the phone waiting for the call that says they are okay. I don't love them less; I just know I am not the one who holds the keys to their lives. And I am grateful for the gift of who they are in my life, and for the gift of being able to hold them more loosely.

It has been seven years now. My life with Creath, the event that took him from me, and the long journey of grief are all a part of who I am today. Surviving has turned into living. Memories have become priceless and ageless. The future is as unknown as ever but is anticipated with open hands and arms.

Somewhere along the way from a plane crash to here I learned some things about myself that have both scared me and excited me. The practical, practiced, and perfectionist side of me began to give way to the dreamer that had been hiding there all along. Slowly, I let that part of me emerge, not knowing that it would keep forcing me outside my comfort zone until the time would come I would no longer recognize the old me.

The word for what was forging the changes inside of me came one day when I was again reading to my grandchildren Leo Lionni's classic book, *Frederick*.[1] As the truth became obvious (at least to me), I leaped to my feet and said aloud, to the children's wondering frowns, "I'm Frederick!"

You see, Frederick is a dreamer. *Frederick* is the story of five little field mice living in a stone wall near the granary that has always supplied them with their winter food. But the farmer has moved away, and the granary is empty. With winter coming on, the mice scamper to gather in the food they would need—all except Frederick.

When they ask Frederick why he doesn't work, he replies that he is gathering in sun rays for the cold days ahead. And again when they question him, he replies he is gathering in colors for the gray of winter, and later, he's gathering words for the long days when they have nothing more to say.

When the food is gone and they are cold and lonely, they ask Frederick about his supplies. He tells them to close their eyes, and as he talks about the sun they remember and begin to feel warmer; when he describes the colors, they can almost see the red poppies in the golden fields. And when he gives them his words, they listen and applaud.

Like Frederick, the dreamer in me began to take some risks, make some tough choices, leave the familiar and the secure. I surprised myself with the painful decision to leave the warm cocoon of the school family I had been part of for twenty-two years. I left among tears. To say good-bye to my office staff and the executive committee who had worked so closely with me the last two years, I took them out to lunch and gave each of them a rosebud, one at a time. I told them how very special they were to me and how very much I would miss being with them every day. To better explain to them—and to myself—why I had to do this, I gave them each a copy of *Frederick* in which I had written what I had come to see inside of me that needed the freedom to grow:

> I'm a dreamer—a reflective thinker. I look at the past and the future and contemplate how they each are part of the moment—and how the moment is part of them both.

> Frederick knew that the sun rays, and the colors, and the words he gathered in would soon be past. He knew, too, they could serve the future in a resurrected way.

> So many times in these last years I have allowed bittersweet memories of "what was" to teach me that the meaning in my life yesterday is now the firm foundation for meaning in my life tomorrow.

And so I dream. And a dreamer is always restless. Always reaching. Always pushing back the horizons in the hope, not of fulfillment and certainly not of contentment, but of meaning.

The dreamer can't live without meaning, without loving, without giving. Something in the dreamer is incessant in its striving for expression. Expression must come, or the dreamer will die.

When the time came, Frederick didn't keep the dreams to himself. He freely and gladly shared them. They made the journey of winter together by each giving what he had to give.

It's the dreams that have kept me alive. The holding tenaciously to the hope and the belief that there would be a time and a means for expression of all I was learning and thinking and feeling in this journey I did not choose.

I am excited. I am scared. I am full of confidence. I am filled with doubt. I have every assurance that God is calling me into a new walk of life. I question daily whether I simply have visions of grandeur.

In this life certainty is a myth. Thus the absolute necessity for faith. And so, in faith, I begin a new, as yet untitled, chapter in my life journey.

I was ready to embrace a new me and a new life. I had come to see life as gift in Creath and in my children, and I had come to see my own life as gift, too; gift with all its sorrows as well as joys, tears as well as laughter, pain as well as pleasure, loss as well as gain, and certainly, gift with its source rooted and grounded in the heart of a loving Father. And only as we see it as such do we hold the package, wrapped perhaps in the drab colors of mourning; then, with trust in the One who gave it, we untie the bow, open the box, and begin to live the gift.

O, Father.
It is so good to call you Father.
We need the love that only you, the perfect Father, can give.
We need the assurance that you, the perfect Father,
*   will not leave us comfortless.*
We need the grace to trust that you will give us life
*   beyond our pain,*
*   whether the life you give is carried on in time and*
*   space,*
or life in eternity with you is begun.

Sometimes it is awfully hard to see life as gift,
*   when a loved one is taken*
*   when a dream is broken*
*   when a relationship is severed*
*   when cherished possessions are lost*
*   when children are rebellious*
*   when security has vanished*
*   when we are facing our own death.*

Lord, only you know the gift hidden in the losses in life.

Only you see the treasures in the darkness,
*   the riches stored in secret places.*

Until you are ready to reveal them to us,
Give us your grace for the waiting.
*   Amen*

16
Making Friends
with Loneliness

This is what the LORD says—
your Redeemer, the Holy One of Israel:
"I am the LORD your God,
who teaches you what is best for you,
who directs you in the way you should go."

Isaiah 48:17

Loneliness is one of the most universal sources of human suf-
fering today. . . . By running away from our loneliness and by
trying to distract ourselves with people and special experiences,
we do not realistically deal with our human predicament. We
are in danger of becoming an unhappy people suffering from
many unsatisfied cravings and tortured by desires and expec-
tations that never can be fulfilled. . . . To live a spiritual life
we must first find the courage to enter into a garden of soli-
tude. This requires not only courage but also a strong faith. As
hard as it is to believe that the dry desolate desert can yield
endless varieties of flowers, it is equally hard to imagine that
our loneliness is hiding unknown beauty.

Henri Nouwen
Reaching Out

I have avoided writing this chapter until the very end. I'm not
sure what I will say. Loneliness is too close a companion for
me to be at all objective about it. It has gone with me on

long walks, sat with me through numerous silent evenings, stood with me in the middle of a group of laughing people, and lay across the bed with me while I cried because I didn't know what else to do. It seems that even when I escape it for a while, it is waiting not too far away. We have had long talks, loneliness and I, and I have to say that I have learned much from our journeying together. We have become friends. But the friendship was a long time in coming.

I can't be philosophical about loneliness. I can't be theological about it. I can only deal with it as experience. And while my wanderings through the subject may not make sense at all to some, to others it will make only too much sense. The trail marked "Loneliness" is indeed crowded with many travelers, all feeling very much alone.

Loneliness did not just come into my life with the accident that left me a widow, but it did become immensely intensified then. I think I have always known a good deal of loneliness because I lived so much of my life inside the shell I constructed to keep out the things that frightened me. The thing I was most afraid of was that if you knew me, you wouldn't love me—so I had to stay close to a hiding place.

Once when the question came up in a small-group exercise, "If you were an animal, what animal would you be?" my answer was immediate: "Turtle. Because if you get too close to me I will pull in my head and my feet and you won't even know I am there."

Years later when that same question came my way, I responded with "Chameleon." I said, "You know, I can be any color you want me to be, and I can be that color so vividly you would never guess I am dull gray."

People-pleasing is a very lonely business. Even so, the loneliness of those days was tempered by being the wife of a man who loved me dearly and the mother of three children who brought us great joy. I loved being a wife and mother and found a great sense of fulfillment in those roles. I certainly experienced loneliness at times in our relationship, but it was always short-lived.

The nature of our lives got us to the place more than once when we realized we spent a lot of time together but often found it hard to connect. Yet deeper than any loneliness I ever felt was the absolute joy of being anywhere Creath was; just having him in sight made my world feel right. And as the years with him turned from two to ten to twenty-seven, I became more and more secure in the love and acceptance he gave me, and the turtle ceased to be. The chameleon, however, was a little more tenacious.

The loneliness that moved in after the accident does not allow for a simple definition. I described it once as an octopus with eight long tentacles wrapped around me; the harder I fought the tighter it squeezed. At times I felt it as a vacuum, a vast dark emptiness of space, void of any recognizable emotion. Other times I heard it as a primal scream reverberating as an echo through the canyons of a dark mountain range. And sometimes it was just silent tears that would not stop.

Even though as I talk about loneliness now I may refer to it as *was,* it often still *is.* But my acceptance of it, and my coming to see that it has many good qualities, allows me to live with it without fighting it as though it were an enemy.

Oftentimes we can look around us, or inside ourselves, and find excuses for the loneliness we are experiencing. Sometimes there is a reasonableness to it. Sometimes it defies all explanation. It is just a sense that something deeper than deep, down where we can't touch it, is trying to tell us something.

Could it be that loneliness is given to us as a reminder that this world was never intended to be our home and the things of this world were never intended to satisfy us? We were made for something far greater than this world has to offer, and when we choose to give our lives to a loving, sovereign God, he will tug at our hearts so we don't get too attached to our toys, whatever they may be. He will remind us from time to time that our real destiny is in him.

Herein is loneliness as a gift. Augustine said it for us: "O Lord, our hearts are restless until they find their rest in thee." No person, no matter how much we love that person, no matter how much he or she loves us, can be our total fulfillment. No amount of earthly happiness can suffice for the longing for the eternal born in our hearts when we become a child of God.

The only true and abiding fulfillment for our lives is found in Jesus Christ, and because we are fully human even that must await ultimate completion in the next life. But the good news is that *even* in our loneliness God is at work to teach us more about who we are, more about who he is and more about what he came to do in our lives—more than we could know if nothing ever drove us inward.

Even so, we do live in this world at present. Things that are meaningful to us cannot be ignored. The need to love and be loved, the need for companionship, the need for a feeling of connecting with someone is a daily part of our existence. When these things are missing from our lives over a long period of time, the resulting loneliness often seems to threaten our sanity. It becomes an ache that feels very much like physical pain, and it goes on day after day after day. Then we will do almost anything to escape it, just for a little while, even when we know it will come back when the pleasure produced by our escape passes.

There is nothing inherently wrong with an occasional soothing balm for the open wound; the danger is in those means of escape that lead us further from ourselves and further from the healing graces that only God can give—and that only in time. Some escapes in themselves are destructive, and others are self-defeating.

How do I keep from being engulfed by the emptiness that often cries out for anyone to please give me a hug? How do I turn my endless nights into occasions for magic moments to happen in my soul? How do I take the silence of my house and let it become a "garden of solitude"? How do I come to see loneliness as a gift I can unwrap and find therein treasures I might never have if I only curse the darkness? How do I keep from running so fast and so hard that I can't feel the loneliness and thus miss the blessing?

I have had seven years to practice, and I'm not real good at it, but I have made some progress. I tried busyness—and still do sometimes, I must confess. I have tried reading voraciously. I have been accused of being permanently attached to my telephone. I have spent hours at a time writing in my journal, being brutally honest with anything I was thinking and feeling. I have begged God to send relief. I have bribed family and friends by cooking for them or by treating them to some entertainment. Although some of these have become self-defeating and some have led to pure fatigue, gratefully, I was able to stop short of searching for escape in more destructive ways. The real danger for me was in giving in to loneliness as a way of life and dying inwardly long before I died physically.

I had to get very angry at the persistence of loneliness before I let it become my teacher instead of my master. As time went on, loneliness became a pain as real as the pain of grief, and equally as paralyzing. I did become angry, angry that loneliness pervaded my whole life like a bad cold that leaves you miserable but not sick enough to go to bed. And I got very tired of the sadness that accompanied it. I yelled into the silence, "Please, God, what am I supposed to do with this? I'm going down for the third time!"

Well, he didn't take it away—he sent me into what I call the laboratory of loneliness. Instead of getting easier right away, the loneliness became vicious. Like the pain of grief, there was no way around it. I had to go through it.

So I again read Scripture with desperation, pleading for some understanding, some way of seeing this part of my journey in relation to my life in his hands. In my searching I found inside of me one last door that, in all of my dealing with the issues in my life, I had avoided opening. It was labeled SINGLE, and when I opened it I found all the things I was sure I couldn't handle. This room frightened me so much I had put a padlock on it, built a moat around it, and stocked the moat with alligators. But alligators don't scare God. So, in his severe mercy, he led me through the treacherous moat and into that room.

Having married young, living alone was something I had never had to deal with. Neither was singleness. I found myself a very reluctant middle-aged adolescent. I can laugh as I write that, but I wasn't laughing when I realized that is exactly what I was. I say "was" because I finally grew up—I think. But it wasn't easy. I was a fairly young widow but definitely an older single living in a world of married couples. I didn't know where I fit in. I didn't try reading books to find out because the books written for singles seemed to be aimed at the under-forty crowd, most of them for under-thirty. I knew I didn't fit there. Marriage books and sermons were definitely for someone else.

I was frightened of my vulnerability, but more frightened to ignore it. There didn't seem to be a map for the maze I found myself in. So I had to stumble through, not knowing what lay ahead.

I filled journals trying to find words for whatever was going on inside of me, trying to name the fears attached to the risk of loving again and the fears of not loving again. In my journals I asked myself questions I couldn't answer.

Did I really want to put myself in a position to lose again and hurt as badly as I have these last few years? Will keeping the door on that part of my life closed protect me? Or will keeping the door closed eventually make me cold and distant? Will opening up to new possibilities with all the uncertainties inherent in new relationships make me more fun for even my kids and my friends to be around, just because I am not being so protective of my feelings? *Will the loneliness ever go away?*

I had learned by now that answers come with living the questions. I knew the cure for my loneliness was not finding another person to spend my life with but in coming to a comfortableness with all that makes me who I am. So I lived the questions. For a very long time, it seemed.

As I struggled long and hard with all the emotions that accompany aloneness, I sometimes felt that God had abandoned me. One time I took a walk in anger and asked him if he really knew what he was doing. I actually questioned him rather severely—perhaps I could even use the word *accused*. I asked him if he was only interested in the big, important events in our lives, like airplane crashes, and if he opted not to get involved in the little, everyday things that seemed, on the surface, rather meaningless.

I was angry because I needed that tiny touch of human companionship I had been waiting for, and then was deprived of through something I felt God could have intervened in had he so chosen. So here I was, walking to gain control of my intense disappointment over what I felt to be God's indifference.

In the midst of a flood of tears I thought of what C. S. Lewis said in the early days of his grieving the loss of his wife, Joy: "Not that I am (I think) in much danger of ceasing to believe in God. The real danger is of coming to believe such dreadful things about him."[1]

Then I heard it—a quiet, gentle voice saying, "Have I been so long with you, and yet you do not know me?" (John 14:9, my paraphrase of KJV). And again, as I had done so many times in the past, I wrestled at yet another level with God's promises, with his love and his wisdom, with his sovereignty and our free will, with his doing what is best for us when we see it differently and plead with him to do it our way. What I was actually wrestling with was whether I was going to trust him with this part of my life too.

Need I tell you that in a short time I came to see that God was right all along? A few days after all this I was again walking and asking God (I think this time with openness to hearing what he had to say and not what I wanted him to say) to please help me understand all I had been going through and why it had to be this way. He met me on that walk, and an intriguing allegory began forming in my thinking. When I got back home I wrote my thoughts:

> There was inside of me a room that for too many years had held something akin to a caged animal. As the animal became more and more aware of its hunger, it began to pace furiously, looking for a way out of the cage. Even though with the longing for freedom came a fear of what might be out there, the hunger kept the animal from simply lying down and accepting the cage as home.
>
> Then one day the Trainer who knew all about the animal allowed the door to the cage to be opened. The surprised animal burst through the door, only to find itself in a larger pen with very little food, and the only opening being guarded by the Trainer himself. The angry animal began to run wildly around the pen, growling insults and accusations, and occasionally lunging toward the opening in hopes that the Trainer would relent and let it out into the spaces beyond. Yet, each time, the Trainer stood firmly in the way, never giving explanation why the animal must stay thus contained.
>
> After some time the exhausted animal began to slow its pace and look more carefully at the food that had been provided, at the realities of true freedom, and at the possible motives of the Trainer for standing in the gap.
>
> Soon the Trainer began to quietly speak. The animal had to be very, very still to hear the words that would bring a sense of peace to its tired and troubled spirit.
>
> > "You may have thought you were, but you were not ready for freedom. Your hunger was too great. You had become so accustomed to the caged way

of thinking and relating that immediate freedom would have destroyed you. You needed some time in a larger arena, but an arena with safeguards.

"Oh, I knew the fences would make you angry. And I knew you would blame me for teasing you with a little food and a little freedom, and for standing between you and what you thought you wanted. But I know you better than you know yourself.

"It had to be this way. You had to be fed slowly so you would later know how much is good for you and how much would be harmful. You had to have time to get used to the new inner compulsions, so you could control them rather than them controlling you.

"You needed me to protect you, not from the one whom I allowed to open the door to your cage, but from yourself. You were too vulnerable to the forces at work inside of you.

"I understood your anger when you yelled at me, and I felt your tears when you cried them. I, too, suffered when I was tempted, and because I was tempted, I am able to help those being tempted.

"So you see, I will stand in the gap as long as it takes for you to become acquainted with the intensity of your passions so long denied. I will let you out into full freedom only when those passions are your servant and are no longer in danger of being your taskmaster."

With that the Trainer stepped aside. The animal felt rather than saw that the boundaries had been removed. It need look no further—for its freedom was within.

And so in loneliness I again saw a wise and loving God at work. He has a purpose in all that he does, in the pains he allows

as surely as the blessings he bestows. He would teach us, as oft
as we need it, that our sufficiency is in him.

> O Lord, who would have ever guessed
>   that you would store such riches in a secret place
>   called loneliness?
> Who would have guessed that in the soil of loneliness
>   you would tuck away the seeds of contentment?
>
> Help us to see that our loneliness is not a feeling to be
>   cursed,
>   but a friend to be listened to.
>
> We so fear loneliness
>   that we cram our calendars full of activities,
> All designed to assure that we will not be alone.
>
> And these distractions become so noisy
>   as they clamor for our attention
>   that we can't hear you tell us that our loneliness
>   is where you would like to meet us
> and remind us that you love us,
>   and that we are really not alone,
>   and that this world is not our final home,
>   and that deep inside ourselves is the cure
>   for our loneliness;
> Not out there somewhere.
>
> The cure is inside ourselves because that is where you are.
> You would have us look inward
>   and see you at work in our lives
>   to show us the rainbow through the storm,
>   the light flickering in the darkness,
>   the smile behind the pain,
>   the hope inside the grief.

*You would open our ears
To hear the laughter we thought was gone,
     the word of comfort we had turned away,
          the whisper of encouragement we desperately need.*

*You would quicken our hearts
     to feel the warmth of the sunshine on our shoulders,
          the assurance of the hope we have as your child,
               the joy of an embrace from a friend.*

*In our loneliness, Father,
     you would open our eyes and our ears and our hearts
     to the wonders of your grace.*

Don't let us miss it.

                         Amen

17
With Open Arms

You turned my wailing into dancing;
   you removed my sackcloth and clothed me with joy,
that my heart may sing to you and not be silent.
   O LORD my God, I will give you thanks forever.

Psalm 30:11–12

Listen to your life. See it for the fathomless mystery that it is.
In the boredom and pain of it no less than in the excitement
and gladness: touch, taste, smell your way to the holy and hid-
den heart of it because in the last analysis all moments are key
moments, and life itself is grace.

Frederick Buechner
Now and Then

It was in the loneliness of my aloneness and in believing that being a widow did not mean my life was over that I learned to listen to my life. When the busyness was stilled and the distractions had lost their appeal, there was just me. And I had a lot to listen to.

I had to listen back to my life, to all those years when I hid in fear from what it might say to me. I had to listen to the good and the bad of it and choose to take only the good forward. I had to listen to the dreams of it and see that they were not lost. I had to listen to the pains that had been forced inward and cry for them, and I had to listen to the joys that had been overshadowed by my anxieties and rejoice that I could

141

still feel them. And in listening back, I embraced the happiness it contained.

I had to listen back to my life in transition, to all those days and weeks and months of grieving, of struggling with a new identity, of learning to live life in new ways, of assuming responsibilities beyond my level of comfort, of allowing my dreams to find expression.

I had to listen forward to my life's tomorrows. And I discovered that I do not fear them. I do not know what lies ahead for me, but I am content to know that the God of my past life is also the God of my life to come.

And so I am striving to listen to my life today. To feel my pains acutely and my joys deeply. To sigh less and laugh more. To think about my feelings and feel along with my thinking. To pay attention when my body and my spirit tell me to slow down before I lose myself again. To hold moments for a very long time so they don't escape before I have lived them. To celebrate the little things that constitute my daily life.

For quite some time after the accident, I looked "out there" somewhere for something to put my life back like it had been before it was so rudely disrupted. I wanted life to feel good again. I wanted that same contentment I had always felt when Creath was part of my everyday world. I wanted the familiar, the security, of what I had always known. And so I searched, until one Christmas I discovered what I was seeking was not "out there."

We had been given the use of a condominium in Colorado for the week. I was sure that getting away from home with the whole family for Christmas was the answer to my blues. Nine of us went, and while it was a special family time, I realized before we left Colorado that if I was ever going to find contentment in my life, it was going to be in my own backyard.

The real answer came four months later, when I celebrated my fiftieth birthday. My three children and my daughter-in-law gave me something that would prove to be the catalyst for opening my life up to holding on to my dreams while living the moment. The gift takes a little explaining: When we were raising our children back in the sixties and seventies and life, marriage, and kids would get a little tedious, I would remind Creath that someday for my midlife crisis I wanted a red convertible. For my rather inhibited personality, a red convertible was the ultimate in expressing a free spirit, which I was convinced was lurking around somewhere inside of me, afraid to come out. I just knew that convertible would release it. So it became the standard joke around our house, that when life was bearing down too hard on me, it was time for my red convertible.

After a rather free-spirited surprise "fifties" birthday party with my colleagues at work, I came home, and in my driveway was a red convertible with the top down, balloons cascading out of the back, and a birthday card on the front seat that read, "You have forty-eight hours to have a mid-life crisis!"

I laughed and I cried as I drove that rented red convertible around with the top down, of course, even in the light April rain. I drove to the airport that night to pick up some friends from Focus on the Family and realized a feeling of freedom completely foreign to me. When we got back to the house, my children and some friends were there, "in my own backyard," with cake and balloons—and finally I knew the contentment I had thought would never be mine again.

My children had no way of knowing that they were giving me back my life. The red convertible had to be returned, but not the things it gave me—the freedom to dream, the daring to live life to the fullest, the permission to enjoy the moment in spite of the temporary nature of things that give us pleasure. It gave me the desire to welcome the ebb and flow of life chock-full of opportunities and responsibilities; it helped me see the privileges of work to be done, things to be learned, sorrows to be grieved, and joys to be celebrated. These things were mine to keep. With that birthday gift came a new way of relating to the life that lay in front of me now. I was beginning to reach out toward life with open arms.

Strangely, it was from this mountaintop that I plunged almost immediately into a valley that staged one of my most intense battles. It was in this valley that I faced, at its deepest level, the question of whether I wanted to get well spiritually and emotionally, because this valley presented some very severe trials.

Luckily, I carried with me into that valley two important things from the red convertible: the understanding that the contentment I sought was to be found inside of me, and the taste of a free spirit that did not depend on a red convertible for its sustenance.

Toward the end of those months of inner turmoil and monumental decisions I read the words of the psalmist and nodded my head in affirmation: "It was good for me to be afflicted so that I might learn your decrees" (Psalm 119:71).

Soon after, I was writing in my journal of the thoughts and feelings that had engulfed me since my grandmother's death a few weeks earlier and of the sudden death of my aunt just days before and of the intertwining of this family that had been drawn together from our distant places through these two losses. I was writing, too, of some things that had weighed heavily on me as I had had to show a toughness with some personal issues that I had not been able to dredge up the year before. I knew my mourning had become dancing when, almost in mid-sentence while recording some very real stresses, my writing changed to this:

Ah, but my cup is so full—I want to tell everyone, "Hey! I made it through the valley!"—I guess I sort of *have* been telling anyone who would stand still enough to listen.

It just feels so good—It is not the painful joy I have felt so much in this long journey—A joy in God's grace, to be sure—But a joy surrounded by the pain of loss.

This joy is the kind that bubbles up from within and

cannot be kept inside—It has to be shared—it has to be shouted and sung and hugged and set free.

I feel I am standing on tiptoe with excitement—excitement over what I am not sure—I think I feel like my life is about to burst open and I will experience things I have never even dreamed.

I don't want to see it all right now—I want to live it, moment by moment, as it comes to me.

I know there is other heartache out there—But I believe there is also love and beauty and awe and wonder—A place to belong and a people to belong to.

And I believe there is good and God and meaning and purpose—And a calling that is mine.

My heart is racing even as I write this, in anticipation of the new threads to be woven into the tapestry of my life—Indeed, even now being woven in as I live these present days with unbounded gratitude.

I love the bright colors in my tapestry today—And I pray that when God sees fit to again weave in some darker threads, he will give me the grace to trust him still.

It has been a long, painful, mysterious, unpredictable, astonishing journey from June 28, 1987, to here. I have cried more tears than I knew one body could hold. I have knelt in awe of God's magnificent grace and his undeniable faithfulness more times than I can count. I have felt anger long denied and joy long unrecognized. I have begged God for answers and thanked him for the trust he sent instead. I have felt his peace on the mountaintop and sensed his wisdom in the valley.

And I have learned that his "Yes" can change our lives just as surely as his "No."

When I asked God to please let me write, I had no idea what his "Yes" would take me through. I didn't know of the painful inward journeys I would have to take and the journeys far outside my feelings of capability and comfort I would be forced in to.

I wrote thoughts and feelings with brutal honesty in my journals, and in the ministry newsletters I wrote of pains and losses and learnings that I knew were common to us all. I begged God for words to attach to the rumblings inside of me. I wrote poems and prayers when the turmoil inside me spilled over and I had no choice but to find a scrap of paper, a napkin, the back of a wedding invitation, a deposit slip from my checkbook—anything so I could write what I could no longer contain. Finding the words for the heretofore nameless thoughts and feelings was a great part of the healing of the griefs and the guilts, and being able to share those words gave me possession of my thoughts and feelings instead of letting them possess me. Words became the wings for my life experiences.

All through the writing of these pages, I have told God that if no one ever sees them but me that will be okay, because I *have* to write. As I have written, I have cried tears of intense sadness as I have recalled pains of the past. I have cried tears of incredible joy as I have felt the ecstasy of living my dream. I have wept with gratitude for what he has brought me through, and still I have looked ahead with expectancy for where he will lead me.

As I write these last words, tears of both sadness and anticipation accompany them. Sadness, I guess, that what I have wrapped my arms around for so long in pursuing this dream will leave me now. Anticipation of what new dream will take its place.

Life beckons me onward now, and whatever it holds, with God's grace and faithfulness I will live it fully alive. And so I close this chapter of my life with words that emerged out of more than five years of praying for the grace to keep choosing to go on each time the darkness threatened to overpower me.

Dreams die hard,
And they should.
But not so the dreamer

Dreams are the stuff that living is made of,
And what keeps us reaching and growing—and glowing.

Dreams are that part of us that hitches to a star
And sprinkles whatever darkness may be with hope.

Dreams are at once fragile and resilient,
    fleeting and persistent,
        comforting and disturbing,
            magnificent and absurd,
                possible and impossible.

They must not be held too tightly,
    for they need room to breathe.
They must not be held too loosely,
    for they need the nourishment of loving attention.

Yet not all dreams were meant to be.
Some serve a higher purpose in dying,
And as with any death,
The survivor often loses heart.

But the dreamer must not die with the dream.
The grieving must become the altar upon which to offer the loss
    and ask for grace to dream again.

And when the grieving has done its purifying work
The dreamer will emerge to find
    that the death of one dream gives birth to another,
Another perhaps in every way more usable in the kingdom.
Yes, dreams die hard,

And they should.
But not so the dreamer

For when God possesses the dreamer,
He will mold the dream,
AND IT WILL BE RIGHT.

Father,
For your marvelous love that enfolds us
    We thank you
For your amazing grace that frees us
    We thank you
For your magnificent power that sustains us
    We thank you
For your unapproachable wisdom in our trials
    We thank you
For your wondrous mercy in our brokenness
    We thank you
For your unspeakable gift of life
    We thank you

Let everything that has breath praise the Lord!
                    Amen

Endnotes

Chapter 3   Strong in the Broken Places
1. Frederick Buechner, *The Sacred Journey* (New York: HarperCollins Publishers, 1982), 46.

Chapter 4   Questions Job and I Asked
1. Max Lucado, *In the Eye of the Storm* (Dallas: Word, 1991), 161–162.

Chapter 5   A Long and Painful Journey
1. C. S. Lewis, *A Grief Observed* (New York: Bantam, 1961), 38, 53, 54.

2. C. S. Lewis, *The Problem of Pain* (New York: Collier Books, Macmillan Publishing, 1962), 110.

Chapter 6   Do You Want to Get Well?
1. See John 5:1–14.

2. "Then Came the Morning," words by Gloria Gaither, music by William J. Gaither and Chris Christian. Copyright 1982 by Gaither Music Company (administered by Gaither Copyright Management) and Home Sweet Home Music. All rights reserved. Used by permission.

Chapter 7   I Believe . . . Help Thou Mine Unbelief

1. Lucado, *In the Eye of the Storm,* 127.

2. Ibid., 126.

3. See Mark 9:14–24 (KJV).

4. Lewis, *A Grief Observed,* 25.

5. Ibid., 5.

6. Ibid., 42.

7. Ibid., 76.

Chapter 8   The Greater Miracle

1. See Isaiah 40:31.

2. John Claypool, *Tracks of a Fellow Struggler* (Waco, Tex.: Word, 1974), 55.

Chapter 9   Peace Not as the World

1. Elisabeth Elliott quoted by Catherine Marshall in *Beyond Ourselves* (New York: McGraw Hill, 1961), 103.

2. Creath Davis, *Lord, If I Ever Needed You, It's Now!* (Grand Rapids, Mich.: Baker, 1981), 88.

3. Claypool, *Tracks of a Fellow Struggler,* 104.

4. Ibid., 104.

Chapter 10   My Child . . .

1. James E. Means, *A Tearful Celebration* (Portland, OR: Multnomah Press, 1985), 76.

2. Ibid, 29.

3. Ibid, 76.

4. Ibid, 25.

5. Ibid, 36.

6. Yancey, *Disappointment with God* (Grand Rapids, Mich.: Zondervan, 1988), 26.

7. Randy Becton, *Does God Care When We Suffer?* (Grand Rapids, Mich.: Baker, 1988), 51, 61.

8. A. W. Tozer, *The Knowledge Of the Holy* (New York, NY: Harper-Collins, 1961), 1, 2.

9. Richard Foster, Retreat at Glen Eyrie Conference Center, Colorado Springs, CO, March 1993. Used by permission.

Chapter 11   In the Hands of the Master Potter

1. Gordon MacDonald, *Forging a Real World Faith* (Nashville: Oliver-Nelson, a division of Thomas Nelson, 1989), 132.

Chapter 12   Too Much for Too Long

1. Bill Hybels, Senior Minister, Willow Creek Community Church, South Barrington, Illinois. From the message "Building Bigger Hearts" presented to a plenary session of The Foundation, Phoenix, Arizona, 1990. Used by permission.

2. Henri J. M. Nouwen, *The Way of the Heart* (New York: Harper-Collins, 1981), 27–28.

Chapter 13   Quiet Desperation

1. Dr. David Allen, *In Search of the Heart* (Nashville: Thomas Nelson, 1993) 115.

Chapter 15   Life Is Gift

1. Leo Lionni, *Frederick,* a Caldecott Honor Book (New York: Pantheon, 1967).

Chapter 16   Making Friends with Loneliness

1. Lewis, *A Grief Observed,* 5.